Practical Airline Service English

Siun Jung · Jeanhyo Ko

BAEKSAN Publishing Co

PREFACE

항공산업의 발전으로 외국과의 교류가 빈번해지면서 글로벌관광시대로 변화가 된 현재, 항공업 및 관광업을 포함한 모든 산업의 국제화가 매우 빠르게 진행되고 있다. 이에 항공서비스업 및 관광서비스업에 종사하고자 하는 학생들에게 영어습득의 필요성이 그 어느 때보다 중요하게 인식되고 있다. 하지만 진정한 프로페셔널 서비스인으로 성장하기 위해 중요한 것은 일반적인 회화가 아닌 서비스 제공자로서의 정중하고 품위 있는 영어를 구사하는 것에 있다고 할 수 있다.

이 책의 목적은 기내 및 공항 내에서 이뤄지는 영어회화 구문들을 다양하게 제시하여 학생들이 해외에서 또는 한국을 방문하는 외국인들과의 자연스럽고 품격 있는 회화를 구사할 수 있도록 돕는 것에 있다.

두 저자는 외국 항공사에서 오랜 기간 승무원으로 근무한 경력을 바탕으로, 실제 항공기 내에서 외국인 승객을 응대할 때 사용하는 실제 영어회화 패턴의 학습에 중점을 두고 항공사 승무원으로서 반드시 익혀야 할 기내서비스 영어회화를 중심으로 이 책을 구성하였다.

이 책은 여행을 출발하여 목적지에 도착할 때까지의 승객의 동선에 따라 시간 순서로 총 7개의 파트로 구성되어 있다.

그 중 1장과 6장은 승객과 항공사 직원 및 공항 직원들과의 대화내용을 다루었으며, 2장은 항공기승무원들의 비행 전 브리핑에 관한 내용을 실었다. 또한 3, 4, 5장과 7장은 승객의 항공기 탑승에서부터 도착지에 도착하여 비행기에서 내릴 때까지의 전 과정에 걸친 기내에서 필요한 영어회화로 구성하였다.

따라서 본 교재를 활용하여 서비스 제공자로서의 영어회화 패턴을 반복 학습한다면 자연스러운 서비스 영어표현의 습득과 동시에 영어실력을 향상시키는데 큰 도움이 될 것이다.

끝으로, 이 책을 감수해 주신 Alicia Trawick 교수님과 책 출판을 위해 도움을 주신 백산출판사의 사장님과 조경연 이사님 및 편집부 직원분들께도 깊은 감사를 드린다.

공저자

차 례 Contents

PREFACE ······ 3

part 1

From Check-in to Boarding gate • 9

1. Check-in at the Airline counter ······ 12
2. Security check & Immigration ······ 13
3. At the boarding gate ······ 14

part 2

Pre-flight duty for cabin crew • 17

1. Pre-flight briefing ······ 18
   1) Introducing yourself ······ 18
   2) About pre-flight briefing ······ 19
   3) The importance of pre-flight briefing ······ 19
2. Ground check ······ 19
   1) Heading to Aircraft(항공기로의 이동) ······ 19
   2) Preflight check ······ 20

part 3

Before take-off service • 21

1. Passenger boarding ······ 23
   1) Greeting Passenger at the Door ······ 24
   2) At the cabin crew station ······ 26
   3) Passenger's request during boarding ······ 30
2. Seating arrangement ······ 32

1) Separated seats ········ 33
2) changing seats ········ 36
3) Double seating(이중좌석 발생) ········ 38

3. Hand-carry baggage ········ 40

1) Carry-on baggage(기내 휴대품) ········ 41
2) Baggage on the seat(좌석 위의 짐) ········ 42
3) Baggage in the overhead bin ········ 43
4) Carry-on baggage and coats ········ 43

4. Emergency exit seat briefing ········ 45

5. Cabin check for take-off ········ 48

1) seat belt(안전벨트) ········ 49
2) Returning seat ········ 51
3) Tray table & Foot rest ········ 51
4) Aisle clear & window shade ········ 52
5) Other situation ········ 53

part 4 En-Route Service • 55

1. Earphone and Towel Service ········ 56

1) Earphone (Headset) Service ········ 57
2) Towel Service ········ 58
3) Towel Collection ········ 59

2. Drink Service ········ 61

1) Drink Service ········ 62
2) Empty Cup Collection ········ 68

3. Meal Service ········ 70

1) Meal Service ········ 72
2) Meal Service / Unexpected situation ········ 76
3) Coffee & Tea Service ········ 82
4) Collection of meal tray ········ 85

4. In-flight entertainment ········ 87

1) Music Information ········ 88
2) Movie program Information ········ 89
3) Problem with Entertainment System ········ 90
4) Cabin preparation for movie. ········ 93

5. In-flight sales ········ 96

6. C.I.Q ········ 103

7. Destination Information ········ 108

1) Flight information ········ 108
2) Destination Information ········ 110

part 5

Landing & Deplane • 115

1. Prepare for landing ········ 117

1) Collection of Headphones & Cups ········ 117
2) Seatbelt, Seat back & Tray table ········ 119
3) Storage of passenger's Baggage ········ 120

4) Returning Passenger's Clothing / Bag ··· 120
5) Other situation ··· 121

2. Disembarkation ··· 122
1) Deplane and Farewell ··· 122
2) Assist passenger ··· 123

part 6 From Immigration to Customs • 125

1. Immigration ··· 127
2. Baggage claim ··· 130
3. Customs ··· 136

part 7 Handling of irregular situation • 139

1. Sick passenger on board ··· 140
2. Aircraft Delay ··· 144
3. Dealing with disruptive passenger ··· 146
4. Extra service ··· 148
1) Passenger comfort ··· 149
2) Other situation ··· 150
3) Aircraft Service unit ··· 152

부 록 In-flight announcement • 155

Practice 정답 • 179

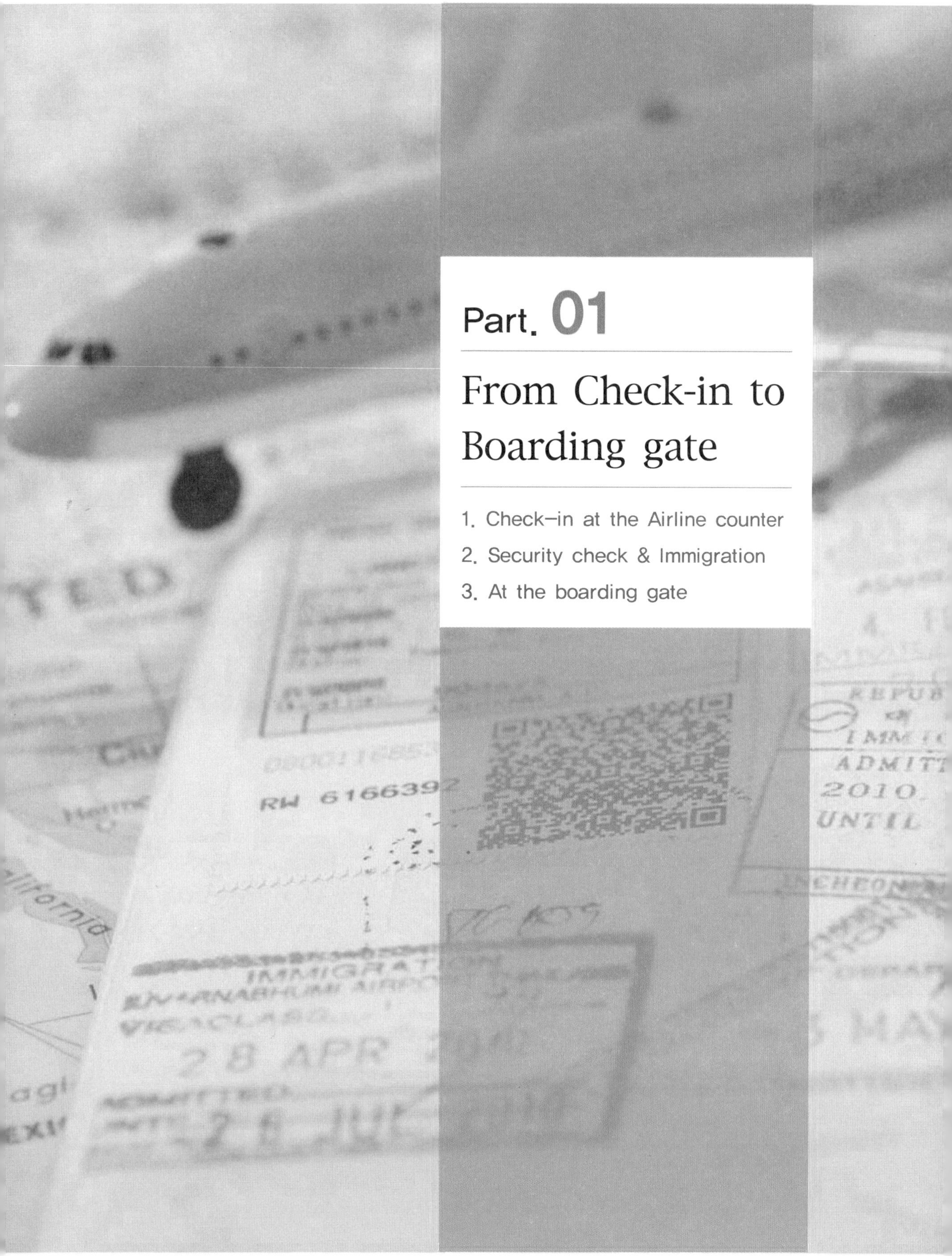

Part. 01

From Check-in to Boarding gate

1. Check-in at the Airline counter
2. Security check & Immigration
3. At the boarding gate

Part 1

From Check-in to Boarding gate

일반적으로 항공여행의 시작은 비행기 티켓의 구입부터 시작이 된다. 인터넷의 발달은 항공사나 여행사에 전화 또는 직접 방문을 통해 구입해야 했던 비행기 표를 간단한 클릭만으로 전 세계 항공사의 티켓 가격을 비교하여 구매할 수 있는 간편성을 제공하였다. 또한 예전에는 왕복 항공티켓인 경우 돌아오는 티켓의 리컨펌(reconfirm), 즉 예약 재확인의 작업이 필수였는데, 요즘은 항공사 자체예약 및 발권시스템의 발달로 항공사 직원의 특별 요청이 없는 한 필요 없는 절차가 되었다.

발권작업도 현재는 인터넷으로 티켓 구입부터 좌석 지정, 탑승권 출력까지의 서비스를 제공하는 항공사도 늘었다. 하지만 인터넷으로 발권을 하였더라도, 공항에서 출입국절차를 위해서는 여권과 출력한 e-티켓은 반드시 지참하여야 하며, 별도로 수화물을 부치는 작업을 진행하여야 한다.

참고: 출입국 절차

일반적으로 출발지 공항에서 이뤄지는 출국 절차와 도착지 공항에서 이뤄지는 입국 절차는 그림 <1-1>과 같다.

출국 시 절차 (Exit procedure)	입국 시 절차 (Entry procedure)
1. 탑승수속 (Boarding Procedure)	1. 입국 심사 (Immigration Check)
⬇	⬇
2. 출국일반대합실 (Departure Waiting Area)	2. 보안검색 (security Check)
⬇	⬇
3. 보안검색 (Security Check)	3. 수하물 회수 (Baggage Retrieval)
⬇	⬇
4. 휴대품 검사 (Carry-On-Check)	4. 세관검사 (Customs Clearance)
⬇	⬇
5. 출국심사 (Immigration Check)	5. 입국 대합실 (Arrival Waiting Area)

그림 〈1-1〉 공항 출입국 절차 순서도

공항에 도착하여 비행기에 탑승하기 전까지 승객의 동선은 다음과 같이 정리할 수 있다.

1. **탑승수속**(Boarding procedure, Check-in) : 항공사 카운터에서의 탑승 수속은 여권과 항공권을 확인한 후 자리를 배정받고 휴대하고 있는 수화물을 비행기에 싣는 등의 작업을 수행하는 단계
2. **출국일반 대합실**(Departure waiting area)
3. **보안검색**(security check) : 공항 및 기내에 안전을 보장하기 위한 보안검색
4. **휴대품 검사**(Carry-on check) : 휴대품 검사 절차는 공항의 규정에 따라 진행여부가 결정됨
5. **출국심사**(Immigration check) : 출국 심사(여권 필요)

일반적으로 승객들은 위와 같은 일련의 과정을 거쳐 면세구역으로 들어가 비행기를 탑승할 수 있는 라운지로 이동하게 된다.

비행기가 도착지 공항에 착륙하여 하기하게 되면 승객들은 해당 국가의 입국절차를 거치게 되는데, 이때 처음 거치는 수속이 입국심사이며, 그 후 각 나라의 보안규정에 따른 보안검색(없는 곳도 있음) 및 수화물 회수과정을 거쳐 세관심사 과정을 거친 후 입국 대합실로 들어서게 되는 일련의 절차를 거치게 된다.

본 장에서는 일반적인 여행의 시작점인 출발지 공항에서 손님과 공항에서 근무하는 직원 간에 이뤄지는 대화를 학습하도록 한다.

Vocabulary

• aisle	• baggage	• baggage claim tag	• boarding pass
• bother	• breakable	• briefcase	• carousel
• check in	• delay	• detector	• metal
• object	• security	• scale	• window

Key Expression

- Good morning. What can I do for you, sir?
- Thank you, enjoy your trip.
- May I see your ticket and passport, please?
- Let me see your ticket, please.
- Do you have any baggage to check in?
- How many pieces of baggage would you like to check in?
- Would you like a window or an aisle seat?

1. Check-in at the Airline counter

항공기 손님들은 여권과 비행기 티켓, 그리고 소지한 수화물을 가지고 이용하는 항공편의 지정 카운터에서 탑승수속(check-in)을 밟게 된다.

Dialogue 1 Check-in(탑승수속)

A Airline staff / P passenger

A: Good afternoon, sir. Show me a ticket and passport, please.

P: Here you are.

A: Are you going to Los Angeles on Flight 002?

A: That's right.

P: Do you have any baggage to check in?

A: Just one,

P: Anything breakable inside?

A: No.

A: Would you put your baggage on the scale, please?

P: O.K.

A: Would you like a window or an aisle seat?

P: I would like a window seat. I hate to be bothered.

A: Here is your boarding pass, ticket and passport. Your seat is 37A window. You will be boarding at Gate number 13. Be sure to be on time, 3:30 p.m.

Dialogue 2 Check-in(탑승수속)

A: Good afternoon!

P: (Putting his ticket and passport on the counter) Hi.

A: Window seat or aisle seat?

P: Aisle seat, please.

A: O.K, sir. How many pieces of baggage would you like to check in?

P: Two. I'll carry this briefcase with me.

A: All right, sir.

(A few moments pass)

A: Here's your boarding pass and this is your baggage tag.
Boarding will begin at 2:20 p.m. at Gate 14.

P: Thank you.

A: You're welcome. Enjoy your trip.

2. Security check & Immigration

Dialogue 1 Security check point(보안수속)

O: Please put all carry-on luggage on the conveyor and take off your shoes.
Step right this way.
Please walk through the scanning device for the security check.
(Beep)

O: Please empty your pockets and go through again, ma'am.
(Beep)

Please step this way, ma'am.

P: What was the buzz?

O: The metal detector has sensed a metal object on you.

Please stand right here for inspection.

What do you have in this pocket?

P: Oh, sorry. Just some keys.

O: That's fine. Thank you, ma'am.

You can go through now.

3. At the boarding gate

Dialogue 1 At the boarding gate in the Airport

P: Is this the gate for Flight 052 to London?

G: Yes, ma'am. May I see your boarding pass, please?

P: Here it is.

G: Thank you. Your seat is 37A, and boarding will begin in a few minutes.

Here is your boarding pass.

P: Thank you.

G: You're welcome.

Practice 1

아래의 문장의 빈칸에 맞는 단어를 고르시오.

aisle / check in / may / boarding / passport / prohibited

1. ______ I see your ticket and passport, Please?
2. How many pieces of baggage would you like to _____ ______?
3. Would you like a __________ or an aisle seat?
4. ______________ will start in a few minutes.
5. I always choose ____ seats because I don't enjoy looking the window.
6. A person needs a ______ to enter and leave most foreign countries.

Part. 02

Pre-flight duty for cabin crew

1. Pre-flight briefing
2. Ground check

Part 2

Pre-flight duty for cabin crew

승무원이 수행하는 업무는 근무순서에 따라 크게 승객의 탑승 전 업무, 탑승 및 이륙 전 업무, 비행 중 업무, 착륙 후 업무 등 4개의 단계로 이뤄진다.

그 중에서 승객 탑승 전 업무는 크게 Show-up(출근), Pre-flight briefing(객실 브리핑), Heading to Aircraft(항공기로의 이동) 및 Pre-fight check으로 나눌 수 있다.

이 중에서 정시에 회사에 출근하는 Show-up을 기본으로, 브리핑에서부터 승무원의 비행 근무가 시작된다고 할 수 있다.

객실 사무장이 주관하는 객실 브리핑에서는 비행할 팀원과의 첫 만남이 이뤄지며, 또한 이 브리핑을 어떻게 주관하는가에 따라 해당편의 서비스 품질이 좌우되기도 함으로 매우 중요한 의미를 가지고 있다.

전 팀원은 한정된 시간 내에 최대의 효율의 서비스를 제공함과 동시에 고객의 만족을 높이기 위해 힘을 모아야 한다.

브리핑에서는 비행에 적합한 복장 및 용모를 갖추었는가와 같은 이미지 점검을 우선 받게 된다. 그 후에는 참가하는 승무원의 명단 및 소개, 각 승무원의 임무 할당과 비행정보, 비행시간, 승객 정보와 같은 정보를 나누게 되고, 비행기의 안전 장비에 대한 점검도 이뤄지며 서비스 절차(기내식 정보, 영화, 기내방송 및 신규 또는 변경 사항)등과 목적지 공항정보에 대한 정보공유도 이뤄진다.

1. Pre-flight briefing

1) Introducing yourself

- My name is ____, pleased to meet you.

- Excuse me, could you tell me your name, please?
- Hello again. How are you? Fine, thanks, and you?
- How's it going? Very well, thanks.
- How are you? Not too bad.

2) About pre-flight briefing

Normally preflight briefing is held on the briefing room or aircraft and the senior crew (usually the purser) introduces everyone and take them through the flight details. Usually this covers the order of the services during the flight, the individual positions and responsibilities for the day, and any special points or passengers with special needs. Security and the aircraft's safety features always get a special mention these days and crew members are sometimes asked one or two questions about emergency procedures.

3) The importance of pre-flight briefing

The pre-flight briefing is important for several reasons.

- To get to know each other
- To be told about the coordination of duties
- To find out the order of service
- To check safety and emergency procedure
- To hear about anything special about the flight
- To hear about the weather en route

2. Ground check

1) Heading to Aircraft(항공기로의 이동)

운항 브리핑은 항공사에 따라 기장과의 합동 브리핑으로 이뤄지는 곳도 있고 별도로 비행기에서 이뤄지는 곳도 있다.

브리핑을 마친 후 승무원들은 공항으로 이동하여 개인 휴대 수화물을 제외한 짐을 탁송하고 출국절차에 따라 CIQ(customs, immigration, quarantine)를 통과한 뒤 항공기에 탑승하여 각자에게 부여된 임무를 수행한다.

2) Preflight check

① 비상장비 및 보안장비 점검

객실승무원은 항공기 탑승 후 각자 배정된 duty에 따라 안전 및 서비스 분야에 대한 pre-flight check를 실시한다. 승객 탑승 전 가지 각각 맡은 바 임무에 따라 담당 구역별로 비상 및 보안장비의 작동 상태 및 정위치 확인을 한 후 그 결과를 객실사무장에게 보고한다.

② 객실점검 및 갤리점검

승무원은 각자의 duty에 따라 담당구역의 갤리 및 객실 내부상태 확인, 화장실 청결상태 및 작동상태 확인, overhead bin 상태 확인, 방송확인, 승객 좌석 및 주변 점검 확인, 좌석 및 life vest 정 위치 장착 여부 확인, call button, reading light, air ventilation 등의 객실 전반의 확인과 비행에 필요한 기물 및 기내식, 각종 객실 용품 및 케이터링 물품 탑재 등을 확인한다.

이때 Meal entree와 tray 개수 확인, Special meal 탑재여부 확인, 기내음료 탑재 및 상태 확인 및 기물 탑재 확인(coffee pot, ice basket, bread basket 등), 각종 서비스용품 탑재 확인(cocktail napkin 각종 mat, 각종 cup, menu card, bag, cream sugar, 등)의 확인은 객실의 점검 못지않게 최상의 서비스를 제공하기 위해 반드시 필요한 절차이다.

③ Pre-flight preparations for boarding

> When cabin crews are on board, they must carry out pre-flight check on emergency equipment, cabin and galley. Make sure there's a safety instruction card in every passenger's seat pocket. Then double-check the number of meals on board, service equipment, stock all the toilets, all of which leaves just enough time to freshen up and get ready to welcome passengers on board.

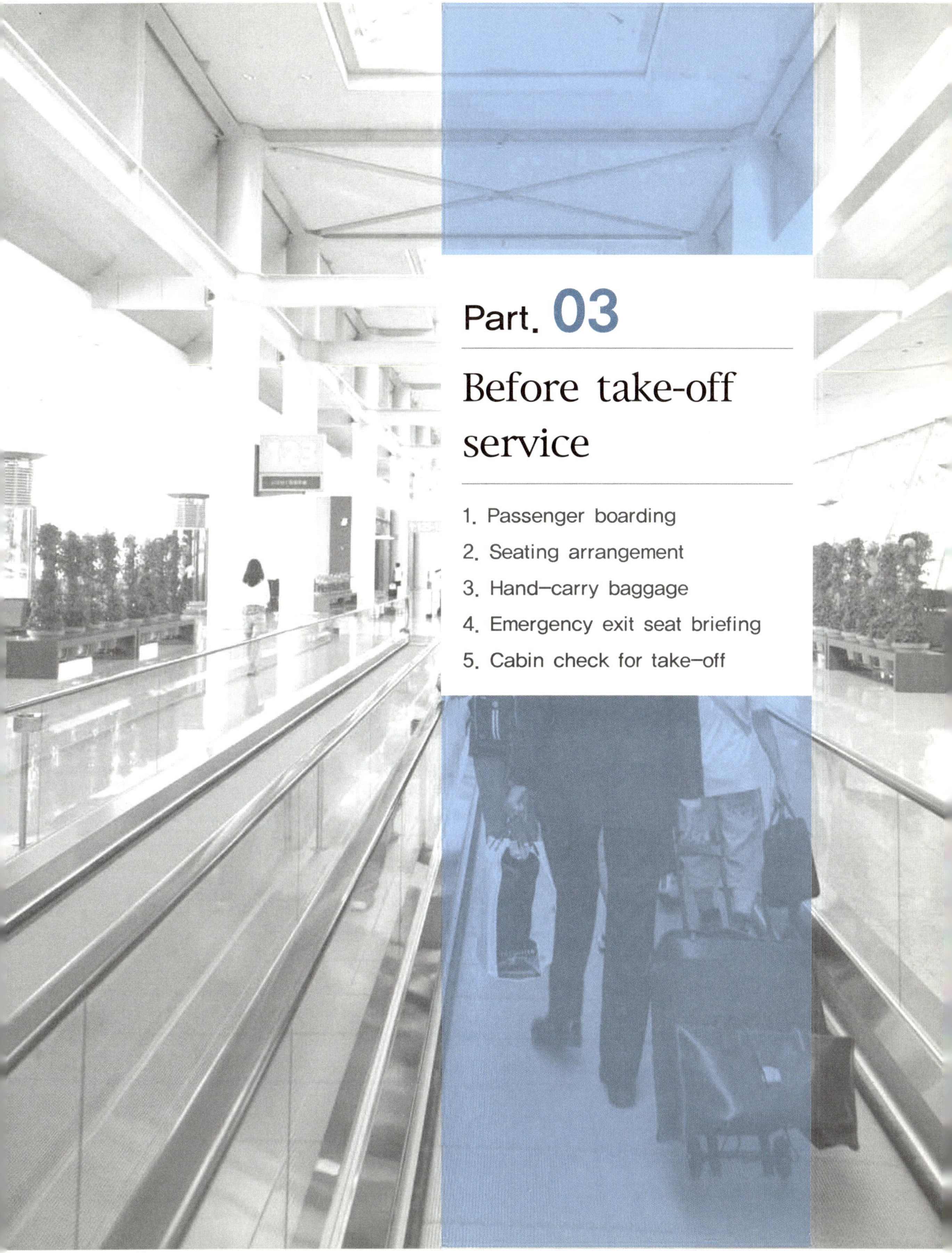

Part. 03

Before take-off service

1. Passenger boarding
2. Seating arrangement
3. Hand-carry baggage
4. Emergency exit seat briefing
5. Cabin check for take-off

Part 3

Before take-off service

비행기 이륙 전 서비스에는 비행기 입구에서 승객들의 좌석을 안내하는 일, 비행기 기내에서 승객들의 좌석을 안내해 주는 일, 승객의 짐을 올바르게 보관하는 법을 안내하는 일 및 이륙을 위해 비행기 기내 및 승객의 안전을 체크하는 일 등이 있다.

Vocabulary

- aisle
- baggage
- bassinet
- bottle(milk bottle)
- bulkhead seat
- cabin crew
- diaper
- formula
- gate
- lavatory luggage
- passenger
- secure
- as soon as possible
- baggage claim
- belongings
- blanket
- cabin
- cargo
- disturb
- fragile
- hurry
- milk powder
- seat belt
- steward / stewardess
- assistance
- bag
- boarding pass
- briefcase
- cabin attendant
- certainly
- flight attendant
- further
- immediately
- overhead bin
- seat number
- stroller

Key Expression

- Good morning / afternoon / evening. Welcome to ______ Airlines.
- Welcome aboard.
- May I see your boarding pass, please?
- Please take this aisle.
- Your seat is in the front of the cabin, on your right.
- It's a window seat.
- Enjoy your flight.
- Have a nice flight.
- May I help you with your bags, sir?
- May I help you with find your seat, ma'am?
- Would you mind putting your bag under the seat?
- If you need anything during the flight, please let us know.
- You're welcome, sir.
- My pleasure, sir.

1. Passenger boarding

승객들이 탑승구(boarding gate)에서 탑승안내를 기다리는 동안, 기내에서는 승무원들이 분주하게 각자의 duty에 따라 비행 준비를 하게 된다. 비행기의 모든 탑승 준비가 완료되면, 지상직원의 안내에 따라 대기하고 있는 승객들의 기내 탑승이 시작된다.

일반적으로 국제선의 기내 탑승은 출발 30~40분 전에 이뤄지며, 국내선 또는 단거리용 소형 비행기일 경우는 출발 20분 전에 탑승이 이뤄진다.

지상직원들은 승객들의 보다 효율적인 탑승을 위해 우선순위를 부여하여 탑승을 안내하게 된다. 1, 2등석의 승객은 일반석과 분리된 전용 탑승구로 출발 전 언제라도 편한 시간에 탑승하도록 안내되며, 임산부 및 영 유아를 동반한 승객, 노약자, 휠체어 승객, 환자, 어른을 동반하지 않고 홀로 여행하는 아이 승객(UM: Unaccompanied Minor) 등은 다른 승객들보다 먼저 탑승을 할 수 있도록 안내를 받게 된다.

일반석 승객의 탑승 안내 시에는 승객들의 불편을 줄이기 위해 좌석번호에 의거, 비행기의 뒤쪽 좌석 승객부터 탑승을 하도록 안내된다.

승객의 탑승은 승객과 승무원들이 처음으로 만나는 접점이므로, 비행기 입구 및 기내에서 승객을 맞이할 때에는 밝은 표정과 상냥한 목소리로 기분 좋은 여행의 출발이 될 수 있도록 하며, 승객의 탑승권에 기재된 좌석번호를 확인 후 왼쪽과 오른쪽을 구분하여 안내하여 빠른 시간 내 모든 승객들이 탑승할 수 있도록 정확한 좌석 안내를 하도록 한다.

1) Greeting Passenger at the Door

Dialogue 1 At the boarding gate (1)

C Cabin crew / P Passenger

C: Good afternoon. Welcome on board. May I see your boarding pass, please?

P: Oh, here you are.

C: Thank you. Your seat number is 50-E. Please take the aisle to the right.

P: Thank you.

C: You're welcome. Have a nice flight.

Dialogue 2 At the boarding gate (2)

C: Good morning. Welcome aboard. Can I see your boarding pass, please?

P: Here you are

F: Thank you. Your seat is 42D, in the back of the cabin on your right.

P: Thanks.

Dialogue 3 At the boarding gate (3)

C: Good morning. ma'am. Welcome aboard. May I see your boarding pass, please?

P: Hello, It's 10H.

C: 10H, Please take the other aisle. Your seat is in the front of the cabin.

P: Thank you.

C: My pleasure. Have a pleasant flight.

Dialogue 4 At the boarding gate (4)

P: (showing the boarding pass) Excuse me. Where is my seat?

C: Good morning, sir. Your seat is over there. Use the next aisle, please.

P: Thank you.

Tip 승객에게 방향을 알려줄 때 쓰이는 표현 정리

1. Please take the aisle to the right / left.
2. Your seat is in the front / middle / back of the cabin.
3. It's over there. Use the next aisle, please

Dialogue 5 At the boarding gate (5) - Passenger with heavy bag

C: Good morning! Welcome on board. Can I see your boarding pass, please?

P: Hi! Here it is.

C: Oh, Excuse me, ma'am. I'm sorry, but I'm afraid your bag is oversized for this cabin.

P: Oh, is that so?

C: Yes. It will have to be placed in cargo.
You can pick it up in the baggage claim area upon arrival.

P: I see. Here you go.

C: Thank you for your understanding, ma'am.

Dialogue 6 At the boarding gate (6) - Passenger with baby stroller

C: Good evening! Welcome on board.
We are sorry but this stroller is a little too big to secure in the cabin. Would you mind us checking it in?
We will make sure that you can claim it at the gate upon arrival.
Please let me help you with it. I will come back to you with your 'Delivery to Gate' tag.

P: Thank you.

What is "delivery to gate" Tag?

- 수화물을 도착지 공항 GATE(탑승구)에서 승객에게 신속히 인도할 수 있도록 조치하기 위한 것.
- 탑승구에서 유모차를 인수하고, 도착지 공항 탑승구에서 인도한다.
- 승객은 "Delivery to gate" Tag을 소지하고 있어야 한다.

2) At the cabin crew station

승객이 비행기 기내 안으로 탑승하게 되면, 객실 안의 승무원들은 각자의 duty zone에서 대기하며 승객의 순조로운 탑승을 돕게 된다. 이때 승무원에게 가장 중요한 일은 승객의 자리를 정확하게 안내하는 일과, 승객이 기내에 들고 탑승한 수화물의 보관을 안내하는 일이다.

또한 특별한 도움이 필요한 승객에게는 별도의 서비스를 제공하도록 한다. 특히 유아를 동반한 승객이나 어른을 동반하지 않은 어린이 승객에게는 더욱 특별한 관심을 주어 편안한 비행이 되도록 서비스를 제공해 드려야 한다.

Dialogue 1 In the cabin (1)

C: Good morning. Welcome aboard. May I see your boarding pass, please?

P: Yes, here you are.

C: Thank you. Please take the aisle to the right. May I help you with your belongings?

P: Yes, please.

C: Would you please put your bag in the overhead bin or under the seat in front of you?

P: Sure.

Dialogue 2 In the cabin (2)

C: Excuse me, sir. Would you mind taking your seat during boarding, please?

P: Oh, I'm sorry.

C: Thank you, sir.

Dialogue 3 In the cabin (3) - Passenger with heavy bag 1

C: May I help you with your bags, ma'am.

P: Thank you.

C: You're welcome. May I have your seat number?

P: Well, It's 43-B.

C: All right. This way, please.

Dialogue 4 In the cabin (4) - Carry-on luggage / Items in the aisle 1

C: Excuse me, ma'am. Is this your bag?

P: Yes. It is mine

C: I'm sorry but we need to keep the aisle clear at all times.
Would you mind putting your bag in the overhead bin or under the seat in front of you? Thank you.

P: I'm sorry. But I can't lift it because I have a back pain.

C: That's alright. I'll help you.

Dialogue 5 In the cabin (5) - Carry-on luggage / Items in the aisle 2

C: Excuse me, sir. Is this your bag?

P: No, That's not mine.

C: I'm sorry to disturb you. Enjoy your flight.

Dialogue 6 In the cabin (6) - Carry-on luggage / Items in the aisle 3

C: Excuse me, ma'am. Do you have any fragile items in your bag?

P: Yes, I do.

C: Well, then would you mind putting it under the seat in front of you? Thank you.

Dialogue 7 In the cabin (7) - assist mother with child

C: May I help you with your belongings, ma'am.

P: Yes, please. Thank you.

C: My pleasure. May I have your seat number, please?

P: It's 12A & C.

C: Thank you. This way, please.
Here you are. These are your seats.
Would you mind keeping your bags under the seat, please?
That's a beautiful girl. She is so adorable.

P: Thank you so much.

C: You're welcome. If you need anything during the flight, please let us know.

Dialogue 8 In the cabin (8) - Bassinet offer

C: Good morning, ma'am. Your hands are full, let me help you with your bags.

P: Yes, please. Thanks.

C: You're welcome. Can I see your boarding pass, please?

P: Here you are.

C: This way, please. Here you are. Would you like to use a baby bassinet later on?

P: Yes, please.

C: Certainly, ma'am. I'll get one for you right after take-off.

(After take-off)

Excuse me, ma'am. Here is your bassinet, pillow and extra blanket.

I'll set it up for you.

This is the safety strap for your baby, and for safety reasons, you need to hold your baby when the seatbelt sign is on. We have baby items such as diapers, bottles, baby food and powdered milk.

If you need anything, please let us know. Have a nice flight, ma'am.

Tip Bassinet은 기내에 탑승한 아기들을 위한 전용침대로, 기내 벽에 장착하여 아기가 누울 수 있는 아기 요람이다. 일반적으로 75cm, 11kg 미만의 유아만이 이용 가능하며, 장소적 제한이 있으므로 사전예약을 해야 한다. 안전을 위해 규정상 이·착륙 때에는 장착할 수 없으며, 또한 기체요동(turbulence)시에는 bassinet 안에 아기를 놓아둘 수 없으므로, 반드시 아기를 꺼내어 안아주어야 한다.

Dialogue 9 In the cabin (9) - Young child

C: Hello, darling! What is your name?

P: Emily.

C: Hi, Emily. What a beautiful name. How old are you?

P: I'm six years old.

C: Oh, six years old? Do you want to play puzzle games?

P: Yes.

C: Okay. I'll bring them for you.

P: Thank you.

C: Here you are. Have fun!

Dialogue 10 In the cabin (10) - Young child / Unaccompanied Minor

C: Hello. May I see your boarding pass? Thank you.
Your seat number is 34A, right here. What is your name?

P/UM: My name is Ashley.

C: It's nice to meet you Ashley. My name is Jean.
Can I help you fasten your seatbelt?
If you need anything during the flight, just push this call button, OK?

P/UM: OK, I got it. Thank you, Jean.

C: You're welcome. Have a good flight, Ashley.

어른을 동반하지 않은 어린이 승객을 UM(Unaccompanied Minor)이라고 한다. UM이 탑승하면 승무원의 각별한 관심이 필요한데, 아이에게 담당 승무원의 이름을 알려주고 좌석벨트 사용법, 화장실 사용법 및 기타 안전에 관한 사항을 브리핑해주고, 도움이 필요하다면 승무원호출 버튼을 누르도록 알려준다. 또한 옆자리에 앉는 승객에게 아이가 어른을 동반하지 않고 혼자 여행하는 아이임을 알려주어, 비행 중 필요한 도움을 줄 수 있도록 부탁하는 것도 필요하다.

3) Passenger's request during boarding

비행기에 탑승한 승객들은 각각 요구하는 바가 다르기 때문에 자신들이 필요로 하는 사항을 비행기에 탑승한 순간부터 승무원에게 부탁하기 시작한다. 이때에는 승객의 탑승 현황을 파악하여 탄력적으로 대응해야 한다. 승객이 계속해서 탑승하고 있다면, 승객의 안내가 우선이기 때문에 승객의 요구사항을 별로도 기억하고, 나중에 다시 돌아오겠다고 말씀을 드려야 한다. 만약 승객의 탑승이 거의 마무리되었거나 한가한 순간이 온다면 손님의 부탁을 받는 즉시 처리해드리도록 한다. 또한 손님의 탑승이 완료되어 비행기가 움직이기 시작하면 안전규정 상 별도의 서비스를 수행할 수 없다. 이때에는 사과와 함께 서비스할 수 없음을 분명히 말씀드리고, 이륙 후 서비스 해드리겠다는 말을 반드시 덧붙이도록 한다.

Dialogue 1 Passenger request (1) - request for blanket

P: Excuse me, Can I have a blanket?

C: Certainly, ma'am. I'll bring it for you. Just a moment, please.
(a few moments pass)
Thank you for waiting. Here's your blanket.

P: Thank you.

Dialogue 2 Passenger request (2) - Drink order 1

P: Excuse me, miss. Can I have a glass of water?

C: Certainly, sir. I'll get it for you right away.
(a few minutes pass)
Thank you for waiting. Here is your water, sir.

Dialogue 3 Passenger request (3) - Drink order 2

P: Excuse me. May I have some water?

C: Yes, of course. But could you please wait until everyone has boarded.
I'll get it for you as soon as possible.

P: Thanks.
(a few minutes pass)

C: I'm sorry to have kept you waiting. Here is your water.

P: Thank you.

C: You're welcome.

Practice 2

아래의 문장의 빈칸에 맞는 단어를 고르시오.

back / mind / lavatory / boarding / cabin / fragile / bags / anything / as soon as possible

1. May I see your ________ pass, please? Thank you.
2. May I help you with your ______, ma'am?
3. It is in the _______ of the cabin on the right.
4. I will serve you a drink _____________ after take-off.
5. would you ________ keeping your bags under the seat, please?
6. If you need ___________ during the flight, please let us know.
7. Do you have any ______ items in your bags?
8. Your seat is in the back of the ________ on your right.
9. I'm sorry, sir. But would you mind using the __________ after take-off?

2. Seating arrangement

비행기에 탑승한 승객 중 가끔 check-in을 늦게 한 경우, 또는 항공사의 사정으로 인해 일행과 떨어진 좌석을 배정받는 경우가 있다. 이럴 경우에는 좌석에 여유가 있는 경우에도 원칙적으로 승객의 탑승권에 기입된 좌석에 따라 정확하게 안내한다. 그 후 일행인 승객들은 가능한 함께 앉을 수 있도록 배려하고, 좌석이 만석인 경우라면 옆 좌석 승객에게 자리를 바꿔줄 수 있는지 물어보는 방법을 사용하여 같이 앉을 수 있도록 배려해 주도록 한다. 하지만, 좌석을 이동하기 꺼려하는 승객의 경우에는 좌석을 옮기길 무리하게 종용해서는 안 된다.

Vocabulary

- accept
- appreciate
- arrange (ment)
- assign
- available
- behind
- bother
- causing
- change
- disturb
- double seating
- empty
- guide
- Inconvenience
- mistake
- occupied
- separate

Key Expression

- Your seat is behind this one.
- I'll check it for you immediately.
- Would you mind changing seats, sir?
- Please come this way, please.
- I'm sorry, but I'm afraid you're in the wrong seat.
- All the seats are occupied.
- There has been a mistake in seating arrangements.
- Would you mind waiting here while I check?
- I'm sorry for the inconvenience, sir.
- We are sorry for causing an inconvenience.

1) Separated seats

Dialogue 1 Separated passengers - 빈 좌석이 있을 경우 1

P: Excuse me, miss. My friend and I were assigned in different parts of the cabin seats.
Do you have any empty seats together?

C: Yes, we have some empty seats in the middle of the cabin. Is it OK for you, sir?

P: That's fine. Thank you.

C: This way, please.
(a few moments pass)
Here you are. Have a nice flight, sir.

Dialogue 2 Separated passengers - 빈 좌석이 있을 경우 2

P: Excuse me. My wife is sitting over there, and we want to sit together. Can you help us?

C: I'll see if it can be arranged, sir.
(a few moments pass)
Thank you for waiting. There are empty seats in the back of the cabin. Would that be alright, sir?

P: Yes, that's great. Thank you.

C: You're welcome. This way, please.
Here are your seats. Have a nice flight, sir.

Dialogue 3 Separated passengers - 빈 좌석이 있을 경우 3

P: Excuse me, miss.
My husband and I have been assigned in different locations.
Can we sit together?

C: Yes, sir. There are some seats available in the front of the cabin.
Would that be all right?

P: That would be great.

C: This way, please. May I help you with your bags?

P: Oh, Thank you.

C: Here you are. Where is your husband sitting?

P: He is over there.
(let the husband know about the seat change)

F: Excuse me, sir. We have some seats available so you and your wife can sit together.

This way, please. Here you are. Enjoy your flight.

Dialogue 4 Separated passengers - 빈 좌석이 없을 경우

P1: Excuse me. My wife is sitting over there.

Is there any possible way we can sit together.

C: Let me check for you, sir.

(a few minutes pass)

I'm sorry, sir, but all the seats are occupied.

Where is your wife sitting?

P1: She is in 34A, just across the aisle there.

C: Just a moment, please. (Go to P2 to ask to change seats)

C: Excuse me, sir. Sorry to bother you.

But we have a couple who has been assigned separate seats.

Would you mind changing seats for them?

P2: No, I don't mind. Where should I sit?

C: Thank you very much, sir. This way, please.

Here you are. I'm sorry for the inconvenience. Thank you again, sir.

P2: You're welcome.

C: Sir, This gentleman is willing to change seats with you.

This way, please.

Here you are, sir.

P1: Thank you. I appreciate it.

C: My pleasure, sir. Have a nice flight.

Dialogue 5 Separated passengers - Not willing to change

P: Excuse me. My wife and I are sitting in separate seats.
Can we sit together?

C: I'm sorry, Sir. I'm not sure if there are other seats available.
I'll see if it can be arranged.
(a few minutes later)

C: Excuse me, ma'am. I'm sorry to bother you.
We have a couple sitting in separate seats.
Would you mind changing seats so they may sit together?

P: Sorry, I don't want to move.

C: That's all right, ma'am. I'm sorry to have disturbed you.
Please enjoy your flight.

P: I'm very sorry, sir.
I'm afraid I was unable to arrange seats for you and your wife.
If there's anything else I can do for you, please let me know.
Again, please accept my apologies.

2) changing seats

Dialogue 1 빈 좌석이 있을 경우 1

P: Excuse me, may I change my seat?

C: Yes, you may. We have lots of empty seats in the back.

P: If possible, I'd like a window seat.

C: Please, come this way, sir.

Dialogue 2 빈 좌석이 있을 경우 2

P: Do you have empty seats in the front of the cabin?

C: Just a moment, please. I'll check it for you, sir.
(a few minutes later)
Sir, we have empty seats in the middle of the cabin.
Would that be alright, sir?
P: Yes, that'll be fine.
C: This way, please.
Here you are. Have a nice flight, sir.

Dialogue 3 빈 좌석이 없을 경우

P: Flight attendant. I want to change seats.
C: Where would you like to sit, sir?
P: In the front, if possible.
C: I'll see if it can be changed, sir.
(a few minutes later)
Thank you for waiting.
But I'm afraid all the seats in the front are occupied.
If you need anything during the flight, please let me know.

Dialogue 4 Passenger seated in the Wrong seats(손님이 잘못된 좌석에 앉음)

P1 : Excuse me, stewardess. I think this is my seat.
C: (to P1) Excuse me, sir. May I see your boarding pass, please?
Thank you.
(to P2) Excuse me, sir. May I see your boarding pass, please?
I'm sorry, but I'm afraid you're in the wrong seat.
Your seat is behind this one, sir. Would you mind changing seats, please?
P2: I'm sorry. Where is my seat again?
C: (to P1) Here is your seat, sir. Have a pleasant flight.
(to P2) This way, please. Your seat is right here, sir. Have a nice flight, sir.

Dialogue 5 Passenger in Bulkhead seat

C: Excuse me, sir. Would you mind changing seats?
A woman with a baby wants to use a baby bassinet.
She needs a bulkhead seat like this one.

P: Okay.

C: Thank you very much, sir. May I help you with your bags?
This way, please. Here you are.
I'm sorry for the inconvenience.
If you need anything during the flight, Please let me know.

3) Double seating(이중좌석 발생)

Double seating은 항공사 측의 실수로 두 명의 승객이 같은 좌석 번호를 배정받은 경우를 뜻한다.

이때에는 양쪽 승객 각각의 탑승권을 확인하여 중복좌석임을 확인 후, 먼저 정중히 사과를 드리고 난 후, 사무장에게 보고 한 다음 지상직원에게 좌석 배정을 다시 받도록 한다.

먼저 탑승하여 착석한 승객은 그대로 그 자리에 앉으시도록 하고, 나중에 탑승한 승객을 승무원 좌석(Jump seat)에서 기다리도록 권유하고, 지상직원에게 좌석을 재배정 받으면 승무원은 승객을 새로운 좌석으로 안내하고 Double seating으로 인한 불편을 다시 한 번 정중히 사과한다.

Dialogue 1 Double Seating 응대 1

P1: Excuse me, miss. My seat is 12A, but someone is seating there.
Can you check for me?

C: Certainly, sir. May I see your boarding pass, please?
I'm sorry, but there has been a mistake in seating assignments.
Would you mind waiting while I check for this?
(a few moments pass)

C: (To P1) I'm sorry to have kept you waiting.
Your new seat number is 47K. Please allow me to take you there.
Here we are. This is your seat, sir.
I'm sorry for the inconvenience. Please enjoy your flight.

Dialogue 2 Double Seating 응대 2

P: Excuse me. Someone is in my seat.
C: Can I see your boarding pass, please?
I'm afraid that there has been a mistake in the seating arrangement.
Would you mind waiting here, ma'am? I'll check it for you immediately.
P: Sure.
C: Thank you for waiting. Your seat is arranged. It's 56D.
This way, please. I'm terribly sorry for the inconvenience.
Have a nice flight, ma'am.

Practice 3

may / arranged / immediately / occupied / mistake / together / inconvenience / let me

1. Do you have any empty seats __________?
2. __________ I see your boarding pass, please?
3. If you need anything during the flight, please ____ ____ know.
4. I'll see if it can be __________, sir.
5. I'm sorry, but I'm afraid all the seats in the front are__________.
6. I'm afraid there has been a _______ in seating arrangements.
7. I'm sorry for the______________, sir.
8. I'll check it for you________________.

3. Hand-carry baggage

승객의 기내 반입 수화물은 원칙적으로 머리 위 수화물 칸이나 좌석 밑에 보관하도록 안내한다. 일반적으로 승객의 기내 반입 수화물 중 가벼운 물건은 머리 위 선반(Overhead bin)에 보관하고, 깨지기 쉬운 물건 또는 무거운 물건은 좌석 밑에 보관하도록 안내한다.

또한 안전 규정 상 비상상황 시 승객의 원활한 탈출을 위해 비상구나 통로 주변이 짐이 방치되지 않도록 하며, 항상 어떠한 짐도 놓여있지 않게 주의한다.

승객의 재킷, 코트 등은 구겨지지 않게 잘 접어서 보관하고, 옷장(coatroom)이 있는 경우는 여권, 지갑 등의 중요 소지품을 승객이 직접 보관하게 안내한 다음 좌석번호를 코트 안에 표시하고 보관한다. 이때 옷장 안에 보관했던 승객의 의류 또는 짐 등은 착륙 전에 승객에게 돌려주는 것을 잊지 않도록 한다.

Vocabulary

- airsick
- allowed
- carry-on baggage
- coat room
- completely
- disturb
- fall out
- hang
- landing
- lavatory
- need
- overhead bin (rack, compartment)
- pillow
- prohibited
- relax
- removing
- run out of
- safety
- seat belt sign
- seem to
- space
- take-off
- valuables

Useful Expressions

- I'm sorry, sir, but we have to keep the aisle open.
- Would you mind keeping your bag under your seat, please? It might fall out during the flight.
- Would you like me to keep your coat in the coat room?
- Would you mind removing valuables from your coat?
- Would you like me to put your bag in the back of the cabin?
- I'll bring you a baby bassinet following take-off.
- Let me set it up for you.
- I'm afraid we have run out of the TIME magazine.
- Here is the newspaper you requested, sir.

1) Carry-on baggage(기내 휴대품)

Dialogue 1 Baggage in the aisle 1(통로의 짐)

C: Excuse me, sir. Is this bag yours?
P: Yes, it is.
C: I'm sorry, sir, but we have to keep the aisle open.
Would you mind keeping your bag under your seat, please?
P: Sure.
C: Thank you. Have a nice flight.

Dialogue 2 Baggage in the aisle 2(통로의 짐)

P: Excuse me, Flight attendant. Where can I put my bag?
It doesn't fit under my seat and the overhead bin is full.
C: Would you like me to keep your bag in the back of the cabin?
P: Would you do that for me? Thank you.
C: My pleasure. I'll bring it to you after we land in Chicago.
Have a pleasant flight.

Dialogue 3 Baggage in the aisle 3(통로의 짐)

C: Excuse me, Ma'am.

P: Yes?

C: I'm afraid you can't leave your bag there.

P: Why not? It's not in anyone's way.

C: No, but it might be. You're sitting next to the emergency exit.

P: So where do I put it? I'll need things in it during the flight.

C: Why don't you put it under your seat, ma'am. Thank you.

2) Baggage on the seat(좌석 위의 짐)

Dialogue 1 Baggage on the seat 1

C: Excuse me, ma'am. We will be taking off shortly.
That may fall during take-off.
Would you mind keeping your bag under your seat, please?

P: No problem.

Dialogue 2 Baggage on the seat 2

C: Excuse me, sir. Is this your bag?

P: No, That's not my bag.

C: I'm sorry to have disturbed you.
Enjoy your flight.

3) Baggage in the overhead bin

Dialogue 1 Baggage in the overhead bin(선반의 짐 1)

P: (Putting a heavy bag in the overhead bin)

C: Excuse me, sir.
Would you mind keeping your bag under your seat, please?
It might fall out during the flight.
(a few minutes later)
That's perfect. Thank you, sir. Have a nice flight.

Dialogue 2 Baggage in the overhead bin(선반의 짐 2)

C: Sir, did you call for an attendant?

P: Yes, I did. I have only one carry-on bag, but there is no space in the overhead compartment.

C: Is there something under your seat already?

P: Yes, someone else put a bag there.

C: Is the overhead compartment completely filled?

P: Yes, completely.

C: Well, let me find a place for you.

4) Carry-on baggage and coats

Dialogue 1 carry-on baggage

C: Would you like me to keep your bag in the back of the cabin, ma'am?

P: No, that's alright. I'll keep it here.

C: Certainly, ma'am. Have a pleasant flight.

Dialogue 2 Handling coats 1

C: Excuse me. Would you like me to hang your coat in the coatroom?

P: Yes, please. Thank you.

C: You're welcome. Have a nice flight.

Dialogue 3 Handling coats 2

P: Excuse me. Can you keep my coat in the coat room?

C: Yes, sir. I'll keep the coat for you.
Would you mind removing valuables from your coat?

P: Okay.

C: I'll place your coat in the coatroom in the front of this cabin.
Please feel free to let me know if you need your coat during the flight.
If not, I'll return it just before landing.

P: Thank you.

Dialogue 4 No space for coat

P: Excuse me, miss. Please keep my coat in the coatroom.

C: Certainly sir.
(a few minutes later)
I'm sorry sir. I'm afraid I can't seem to find a space for your coat.
Would you mind if I put it in the overhead bin?

P: Okay.

Practice 4

aisle / keep / taking off / under / pleasant / hang / like

1. I'm sorry, sir, but we have to keep the ______ open.
2. Would you like me to ______ your coat in the coat room?
3. Would you like me to ______ your bag in the back of the cabin?
4. Would you mind keeping your bag ______ your seat, please?
5. Have a ______ flight.
6. Would you ______ me to keep your bag in the back of the cabin?
7. We will be ______ shortly.

4. Emergency exit seat briefing

항공사에서 비행기 비상구 좌석은 비상사태 시 승무원을 도와서 다른 승객의 탈출을 돕는 일 등을 하는데 동의한 승객에게 우선 배정되는 좌석으로, 노약자, 어린이, 환자등과 같은 승객에게는 배정되지 않는 좌석이다. 만약 비상구 좌석에 노약자 또는 어린이와 같은 부적합한 승객이 좌석을 배정받았을 경우에는 좌석을 다시 재배정 받는 작업을 거쳐야 하며, 착석승객에게는 비상시의 행동 요령에 대해 별도의 안내를 한다.

Vocabulary

- aviation
- emergency
- evacuation
- exit
- instructions
- in case of
- responsibility
- row

Key Expression

- Please refer to this passenger safety briefing card for more information.
- Please read carefully this safety information card.
- Will you help us as I told you?
- Will you help me in case of emergency?
- Let me change the seat for you.

Dialogue 1 Emergency exit row

C: Excuse me, sir. You are sitting in the emergency exit row.
Please do not open the emergency exit door unless the flight attendant instructs you to do so.
Are you willing to help us in the event of emergency evacuation?

P: Sure. What would I have to do?

F: You'd have to help the cabin crew evacuate the aircraft.
Please refer to this passenger safety briefing card for more information.

P: Okay.

F: Thank you.

Dialogue 2 Emergency exit row

C: Excuse me sir. Are you informed about Emergency exit seat?

P: Yes. I'm.

C: You're now seated on Emergency exit seat and this is the emergency exit door.
The passenger in the emergency exit seat should help flight attendants to evacuate passenger in case of emergency.
Will you help me in case of an emergency?

P: Yes. I will.

C: Thank you sir. Please carefully read this safety information card.
It explains the exit seat and exit responsibilities.
If you have any questions, please let me know.

Dialogue 3 | If passenger does not agree

P: No, I don't want to take this seat.

C: I see, sir. In that case, we need to rearrange a passenger who is willing to take on the responsibility, since this is required by law.
Let me change the seat for you.

IF YOU ARE ASSIGNED AN EXIT ROW SEAT

You may be asked to assist our crew members in the event of an emergency.
You may be required to follow the direction of our crew members to perform the following tasks.
Keep other passengers clear of the emergency exit door until crew members securely open it.
After evacuating, assist other passengers coming down the emergency slide.
Direct other passengers to evacuate away from the aircraft immediately.
Others (Crew members will instruct the task when it is necessary)
Please read the safety instructions leaflet in your seat pocket at your earliest convenience after boarding. Thank you.

Practice 5

rearrange / help / change / informed / told / states

1. Are you ________ to help us?
2. Let me ________ the seat for you.
3. Are you __________ about Emergency exit seat?
4. Will you _______ me in case of an emergency?
5. Please ______ to this passenger safety briefing card for more information.

5. Cabin check for take-off

항공기가 출발을 위해 문을 닫고 활주로로 이동을 시작하게 되면 승객들의 비상상황에 대한 안내 방송이나 행동요령에 대한 시범이 이루어진다. 그 후 승무원들은 이륙 전에 승객의 안전사항을 확인하고 유동물질 고정 및 항공기내 시설물의 상태를 점검하고 승무원도 지정된 좌석(Jump seat)에 착석해서 좌석벨트를 착용한다.

이륙 전 기내에서 이뤄져야 하는 체크사항에는 전 승객의 착석 및 좌석벨트의 착용 여부, 좌석 등받이, Tray table, Arm rest 등의 원위치 상태를 확인하는 것 등이 있다.

또한 승객의 휴대 수화물 및 유동물건의 고정여부, 비상구주변 정리, 수하물 선반의 닫힘 상태, 전자제품 사용 안내 및 확인 등도 필수로 이뤄져야 한다.

Vocabulary

- Captain
- close
- comfortable
- fasten
- fold
- footrest
- hold-up
- magazine
- newspaper
- pillow
- recline
- regulation
- return
- run out of
- safety
- seat back
- toy
- tray table
- turn off
- unfasten
- upright position
- window shade

Key Expression

- Would you mind fastening your seat belt, please?
- Please fasten your seatbelt now.
- Could you please bring your seat back to the upright position?
- Would you please open your window shade for take-off.
- We will be taking off shortly.
- We are going to take off soon.
- Would you mind folding your tray table, please?
- Would you mind returning your seat back to the upright position?
- Would you mind opening your window shade, please?

1) seat belt(안전벨트)

Dialogue 1 Seat belt 1

P: (seat belt not fastened)

C: Excuse me, sir.
Would you mind fastening your seat belt, please?
We will be taking off shortly.
Thank you. Have a pleasant flight.

Dialogue 2 안전벨트 착용을 원하지 않는 손님의 경우 1

C: Excuse me, sir. Would you mind fastening your seat belt, please?

P: I don't like fastening the seat belt. Don't worry.

C: I'm sorry, sir.
But I must ask you to fasten your seat belt before take-off.
It is for your safety and the safety of other passengers.
You can unfasten your seatbelt after take-off, when the captain turns off the seatbelt sign.

Dialogue 3 안전벨트 착용을 원하지 않는 손님의 경우 2

C: Excuse me, sir. Would you mind fastening your seat belt, please?
We will be taking off shortly. Thank you.

P: I don't like to do that.

C: Oh. But, I must ask you to fasten your seat belt for take-off.
It's an airline regulation.
After take-off, you can unfasten your seat belt.

Dialogue 4 안전벨트 착용 법을 모르는 손님의 경우

P: Excuse me. Will you show me how to fasten my seat belt?

C: Of course, sir. Pull it this way.
If you need any help, just press this call button.

P: Thank you.

C: You're welcome.

Dialogue 5 어린이의 안전벨트 착용 1

C: Hi, Let me put this pillow under your seatbelt.
It will be more comfortable for you.
That's better, isn't it?
OR

C: May I put this pillow under your seatbelt? It'll be more comfortable.

Dialogue 6 어린이의 안전벨트 착용 2

C: Hi! What's your name?

P: Brandon.

F: What a nice name, Brandon.
Well, if you fasten your seatbelt, I'll bring you a toy.
Will you do that? Thank you.
(to parents)

F: Ma'am, please hold your child if he doesn't want to fasten his seatbelt.
Thank you.

2) Returning seat

Dialogue 1 좌석원위치 1

C: Please fasten your seat belt.

P: (Fasten the seat belt)

C: Could you please bring your seat back to the upright position for take-off, please?

P: Is this all right?

C: Sure. Please put your bag under the seat in front of you. Thank you.

Dialogue 2 좌석원위치 2

C: Excuse me, ma'am.
Would you mind returning your seat back to its original position for take-off, please?

P: Sure.

C: Thank you, sir.

3) Tray table & Foot rest

Dialogue 1 Tray table 1

C: Excuse me, ma'am.
Would you mind closing (or folding) your tray table (for take-off), please.

P: O.K.

C: Thank you, ma'am.

Dialogue 2 Tray table 2

C: Excuse me, sir.
Would you please close your tray table until after take-off?
We'll be taking off soon. Thank you.

Dialogue 3 Foot rest

C: Excuse me, sir. Would you mind putting away your footrest for take-off?
Thank you.

4) Aisle clear & window shade

Dialogue 1 Aisle clear

C: Excuse me, sir. May I put this in the overhead bin for you?
We have to keep the aisle open.
P: Sure.
C: We are going to take off soon. Please fasten your seatbelt.

Dialogue 2 Window shade

C: Excuse me, Ma'am.
Would you please open your window shade for take-off.
P: OK.
C: Thank you, ma'am.

5) Other situation

Dialogue 1 Drink order 1

P: Excuse me, I would like to order a drink.

C: Sir, we can't serve drinks now. We are about to take-off.

P: Oh, I would really like one now.

C: I will serve you a drink as soon as possible after take-off.

P: O.K.

C: Sorry, sir. But take-off is in just a few minutes. Please bear with us.

P: Thank you.

Dialogue 2 lavatory

P: Can I use the lavatory now?

C: I'm sorry, sir. But would you mind using the lavatory after take-off?

P: I can't wait.

C: All right, but please hurry. We'll be taking off soon.

Dialogue 3 Passenger stand-up

C: Excuse me, sir. Please sit down.
We are taking off now. Please sit in your seat and fasten your seatbelt.
Thank you for your cooperation.

Dialogue 4 Door close 후 휴대전화 사용

C: Excuse me sir. It must be an urgent thing.
However, using your cellular phone in the cabin could affect the safe operation of this flight.

Would you mind turning off your phone to ensure our safety?
Thank you for your understanding.

Practice 6

upright position / regulation / push / fastening / under / open returning / closing / must ask

1. Would you mind ________ your seat belt, please?
2. Would you mind ________ your seat back to the __________ for take-off, please?
3. Would you mind ________ your tray table for take-off.
4. But I ________ you to fasten your seat belt for take-off.
5. Would you please ______ your window shade for take-off.
6. Let me put a pillow ______ your seatbelt.
7. It is an airline _______.

Part. 04

En-Route Service

1. Earphone and Towel Service
2. Drink Service
3. Meal Service
4. In–flight entertainment
5. In–flight sales
6. C.I.Q
7. Destination Information

Part 4

En-Route Service

En-route service란 항공기가 이륙하여 적정고도에 이르러 승객들에게 기내식, 기내 엔터테인먼트(In-flight entertainment), 면세품 판매 등의 여러 가지 객실 서비스를 제공하는 것으로, 목적지에 도착하기 전까지 객실 승무원의 비행 중의 업무를 말한다.

서비스 절차와 내용, 방법은 항공사마다 다르며, 항공사 안에서도 노선별로 서비스의 차이가 있다.

승객에게 최상의 서비스를 제공하는 것도 물론 중요하지만, 항공사 기내서비스는 승객의 안전이 최우선 되어야 한다는 점을 명심하도록 한다.

1. Earphone and Towel Service

항공기 이륙 후 안전벨트 표시등이 꺼지면 승객을 위한 Earphone (Headset) 및 Towel 서비스가 시작된다. Towel 서비스는 각 항공사 마다, 노선과 출발 시간에 따라 서비스 하는 타월의 종류가 다를 수 있다. 일반적으로 중장거리 노선에서는 이륙 후 Hot towel을 서비스하는 경우가 대부분이며, 이때 미리 준비된 Towel에 뜨거운 물을 부어 서비스 직전 온도, 습도 등을 체크한 다음 Towel tong으로 집어서 서비스한다. 아울러 Disposable towel은 항공기에 탑재되어 있는 상태 그대로 승객수에 맞춰 준비한 후, 손으로 하나씩 집어서 승객들에게 제공하면 된다. 참고로, First class와 Business class의 경우는 두께가 있는 Cotton towel로 서비스한다.

Towel service와 Towel collection이 끝나고 나면 음료서비스가 시작된다.

Vocabulary

- be able to
- be careful
- buy
- charge
- earphones (headset)
- finish
- free
- hot towel
- refreshing
- rest
- serve
- use

Key Expression

- Would you care for a hot towel?
- It's very hot.
- It's very refreshing.
- Please be careful.
- Are you finished with your towel?
- May I take your towel, please?
- Would you like to use it?
- Did you have a good rest?
- Would you care for an earphone set?
- It's free of charge.

1) Earphone (Headset) Service

Dialogue 1 Earphone service 1

C: Excuse me, sir. Here are your earphones.

P: Thank you. Do I have to pay for them?

C: No, sir. It's free of charge.

Dialogue 2 Earphone service 2

C: Excuse me. Would you like to have an earphone set?

P: Yes, please.

C: Here you are.

Dialogue 3 Earphone service 3

C: Excuse me. Would you care for a headset?

P: Do you charge for it?

C: No, sir. It's free.

P: Okay. Then I'll have one.

C: There you are. Have a nice flight.

2) Towel Service

Dialogue 1 Towel service 1

C: Would you care for a hot towel?

Please be careful. It's very hot.

P: Thank you.

Dialogue 2 Towel service 2

C: Excuse me, sir. Would you like to use a hot towel?

We'll be serving lunch soon.

P: Oh. I see. Thank you.

Dialogue 3 Towel service 3

C: Hot towel for you, sir?
Please be careful, It's very hot, sir.

P: thank you.

Dialogue 4 Towel service 4

C: Would you like to have a hot towel, ma'am?
It's very refreshing.

P: Thank you.

Dialogue 5 Sleeping Passenger Towel Service

C: Did you have a good rest?
I couldn't serve the towel because you were sleeping.
Would you like to have one now?

P: Sure. I'll take one. Thank you.

C: Here you are.

3) Towel Collection

Dialogue 1 Towel collection 1

C: Excuse me, sir. Are you finished with your towel?

P: Yes, Thank you.

C: (Taking towel) You're welcome, sir.

Dialogue 2 Towel collection 2

C: Are you finished with your towel, ma'am?

P: Yes, I am.

C: May I collect your towel?

P: Yes, please.

C: My pleasure.

Dialogue 3 Towel collection 3

C: Excuse me. Can I take your towel, please?

P: Yes, thanks.

C: You're welcome.

Dialogue 4 Towel collection 4

C: May I take it away? (pointing towel)

P: Yes, please.

Practice 7

free / use / would / finish / may / with / rest / care / charge

1. Are you ______ _____ your towel?
2. _____ I take your towel?
3. Did you have a good _____?
4. ______ you _____ for a hot towel?
5. Would you like to ____ it?
6. Do you ______ for it?
7. It's _____ of ______.

2. Drink Service

Drink service 또한 항공사에 따라 서비스 방법에 차이는 있으나 대체적으로 출발시간과 비행시간(단, 중장거리 비행)마다 조금씩 차이가 있다. 일반적으로 Towel service가 끝나면 Serving cart / Drink cart(중장거리 노선) 또는 Serving tray(단거리 노선)를 이용해 음료를 제공한다.

장거리 노선의 경우 2차 Meal service시에는 Towel service 후 Tray base로 음료를 서비스한 후 Meal service를 한다.

승객들에게 음료를 제공할 때 중요한 점은 시원한 음료는 시원하게, 뜨거운 음료는 뜨겁게 서비스되어야 한다는 점이다. 항공사마다 Drink cart에 음료들이 탑재되어 Chilling이 되기도 하지만 Galley담당 Duty를 맡은 승무원이 주스, 탄산음료, 물, 백포도주 등의 음료를 얼음을 이용해서 Chilling 해야 하기도 한다.

Drink cart로 음료서비스 시 Juice, Soft drink, Alcohol drink를 같이 서비스하는 것이 일반적이다. 이때 승무원은 음료 및 주류 종류와 더불어 칵테일 제조에 대한 충분한 지식이 있어야 한다.

음료서비스 시에는 승객에게 냅킨과 애피타이저 역할을 하는 땅콩 또는 아몬드 등을 승객에게 먼저 제공한 후 음료를 드리도록 한다.

Vocabulary

- add
- alcohol
- as well as
- certainly
- cream
- diet
- drink
- else
- including
- inconvenience
- juice / soft drink
- peanuts
- selection
- strong
- sugar
- tea
- weak
- whisky / scotch / beer / wine / martini / vodka / gin

Key Expression

- Would you like something to drink?
- Can I get you something to drink?
- What would you like to drink?
- Would you care for something to drink?
- Would you like to have something to drink?
- What kind of juice do you have?
- Here is your orange juice. Enjoy your drink.
- How would you like your coffee?
- We have soft drink, juices as well as selection of wine and alcohol.
- Is that all you have?
- My drink is too strong/weak.
- I'm sorry for the inconvenience.
- I'm afraid I don't know that drink. Could you tell me how it's made?

1) Drink Service

Dialogue 1 Drink service 1

C: Would you like something to drink?

P: What do you have?

C: We have juice, soft drinks and some alcohol.

P: What kind of juice do you have?

C: We have orange, apple, grapefruit and tomato juice.

P: Apple juice please.

C: Here you are.

P: Thank you.

C: You're welcome.

Dialogue 2 Drink service 2

C: Good afternoon, sir. Can I get you something to drink?
We have a selection of juices, soft drinks, beer, hard liquor and some cocktails are available.

P: What kind of beer do you have?

C: We have Heineken, Cass and Hite.

P: I'll have a Heineken, please.

C: Certainly. Here is your beer. Enjoy your drink.

Dialogue 3 Drink service 3

C: Good evening, sir. What would you like to drink?
We have juice, soft drinks, whisky and beer.

P: Do you have vodka?

C: Yes, we do. How would you like your vodka?

P: Vodka with orange juice, please.

C: Certainly. Just a moment, please.
Here is your Screwdriver. Enjoy your drink.

Dialogue 4 Drink service 4

C: Would you like something to drink?

P1: Yes, I'll have an orange juice, please.

C: Certainly, ma'am. Here is your orange juice.
(to next passenger) What about for you, sir?

P2: I'd like to have a diet Pepsi, please.

C: We have diet coke only, would that be all right?

P2: That's O.K.

C: Here you go. Enjoy your drink.

Dialogue 5 Drink service 5

C: Would you like something to drink?
We have orange, apple and tomato juice, soft drinks, coffee and tea.
What would you like?

P: Yes, I'll have a cup of coffee.

C: How would you like your coffee?

P: I will have coffee with cream, please.

C: Here you are. Enjoy your drink.

Dialogue 6 Drink service 6

C: Good evening, sir. Would you care for something to drink?
We have juice, soft drinks, beer, coffee and tea.

P: Is that all you have?

C: No, sir. What would you care for, sir?

P: Can I have a glass of whisky on the rocks?

C: Sure, just a moment please. Here is your whisky.
Enjoy your drink, sir.

P: Thank you.

Dialogue 7 Cocktail is too strong

P: Excuse me. My drink is too strong.

C: I'm sorry, sir. I'll add some more tonic water.
How is it now?

P: It's much better now.

C: I'm sorry for the inconvenience. Enjoy your drink, sir.

Dialogue 8 Cocktail is too weak

C: How is your Bloody Mary?

P: It's too weak.

C: I'm sorry, ma'am. If you don't like, shall I add more Vodka?

P: Yes, please.

C: Here you are. How is it now?

P: That's much better. Thank you.

C: You're welcome. Enjoy your drink ma'am.

Dialogue 9 Request not available Drink 1

C: Good evening, ma'am.
Would you care for something to drink?

P: Do you have mango juice?

C: I'm sorry, But I'm afraid we don't have mango juice on board.
We only have orange, pineapple and tomato juice.
What would you care for, ma'am?

P: I'll have tomato juice, then.

C: Sure. Here is your tomato juice.
Enjoy your drink, ma'am.

Dialogue 10 Request not available Drink 2

C: Hello. Can I get you something to drink, sir?
We have juice, soft drinks and some alcoholic drinks.

P: Hmm, Do you have sparkling wine?

C: I'm sorry, we don't serve sparkling wine on this flight.

P: That's too bad. I'll have a Campari with orange juice, then.

C: Certainly. Here is your drink. May I get you more peanuts?

P: Yes, that would be good.

C: Here you are. Enjoy your drink, sir.

Dialogue 11 Request the unknown cocktail

C: Would you care for something to drink?

P: Could I have a Daiquiri, please?

C: I'm afraid I don't know that drink.
Could you tell me how to make?

P: Sure. It's made of rum, lemon juice and some sugar.

C: I'm sorry. But we don't have lemon juice on board.
Is there anything else you would like?

P: Ok. Then, let me have a gin and tonic?

C: Certainly, here is your drink. Would you like anything else?

P: No, Thank you.

C: I'm sorry for the inconvenience. Enjoy your drink.

Dialogue 12 Drink (Beverage) Refill 1

P: Excuse me, could I have another drink?

C: Certainly, sir. What were you drinking?

P: I had a bourbon whisky with coke.

C: Alright, sir. Just a moment, please.
Here you are.
May I take your empty glass?

Dialogue 13 Drink (Beverage) Refill 2

C: Excuse me, ma'am.
Would you care for another drink before dinner?

P: What kind of beer do you have?

C: We have Korean beer: Hite, Cass, and Max.
We also have Foster's.
Which one would you prefer?

P: I'd like Cass, please.

C: Sure. Here you are. Enjoy your drink.

Dialogue 14 Spilled drink on passenger 1

C: Oh! I'm so sorry. Let me get something to clean that up.

P: No worries. I can manage it.

C: Please accept my apologies.

P: I'm fine. Don't worry.

C: Again, I'm very sorry, sir.

Dialogue 15 Spilled drink on passenger 2

F: I'm terribly sorry, ma'am. I'll get something to wipe it up.
May I wipe it up for you?

P: No, that's all right. I can handle it.

F: Please accept my apology. We have a cleaning coupon to compensate.
Would you please accept it ma'am?
I'm terribly sorry.

Practice 8

care for / cup of / like / selection / would / how / weak / inconvenience / afraid/ all / kind

1. Would you ____ something to drink?

2. What _____ of juice do you have?

3. What _________ you like to drink?

4. Would you _______ _____ something to drink?

5. I will have a ______ _____ coffee, please.

6. ______ would you like your coffee?

7. Is that _____ you have?

8. My drink is too _______. Please add some more vodka.

9. I'm sorry for the _______________.

10. I'm _____ I don't know that drink. Could you tell me how to make?

2) Empty Cup Collection

음료서비스가 끝나면 승객들에게 Second offer (refill)를 하고 컵 회수 시에는 "다 드신 컵 치워드리겠습니다(Are you finished with your drink? May I take your cup?)"라고 말씀드린 후 collection하도록 한다.

Vocabulary

- fresh
- in preparation for
- prior to
- quite
- refill

Key Expression

- Have you finished with your drink?
- Did you enjoy your drink?
- May I take your cup/glass?
- Would you care for another drink?
- Would you care for a refill?
- We'll be landing very soon.

Dialogue 1 Passenger finished with the drink 1

C: Excuse me, sir. Are you finished with your drink?

P: Yes, I'm finished.

C: (taking glass) Thank you.

Dialogue 2 Passenger finished with the drink 2

C: Did you enjoy the drink?

P: Yes, I did.

C: Would you care for another one?

P: No, thanks. I'm fine.

C: Then, may I take your glass, ma'am?

P: sure.

Dialogue 3 Passenger finished with the drink 3

C: Excuse me, sir. Are you finished with your drink?

P: Yes, I'm finished.

C: Would you care for another one?

Dialogue 4 Passenger not finished with the drink

C: Excuse me. Have you finished your drink?

P: No, I haven't finished yet.

C: Oh, I'm sorry. Enjoy your drink, sir.

Dialogue 5 Bar closed prior to landing

P: Excuse me. Can I have another drink?

C: I'm sorry ma'am.
We'll be landing very soon and the bar has closed in preparation for landing.

Practice 9

another / take / enjoy / preparation / yet

1. May I _____ your glass?
2. Would you care for _________ drink?
3. No, I'm not finished _____.
4. Did you your drink?
5. We have closed the bar in ______________ for landing.

3. Meal Service

대부분의 항공사들이 노선별로 서양식과 더불어 목적지 나라의 특색에 맞는 기내식을 선보이고 있다. 예를 들어, 한국에 취항하는 외국항공사의 경우에도 식사서비스 시 서양식 Main meal / Entree 또는 비빔밥이나 다른 한식 종류의 Main meal / Entree 중 선택할 수 있게 제공하고, 이때 한식 Tray에는 고추장 또는 김치가 같이 서비스되기도 한다.

Meal service시 가장 중요한 것은 주 요리가 승객에게 서비스될 수 있는 적절한 온도로 오븐에서 Heating되어야 한다는 점이다. 주 요리의 종류에 따라 Heating하는 시간이 조금씩 차이가 있으므로 서비스 시점에 맞게 항공사의 Manual에 따라 준비하도록 한다. 아울러 First class나 Business class의 경우에는 승객들에게 Menu card가 제공되지만, 대부분의 항공사들이 Economy class에서는 Menu card

가 제공되지 않는다. 따라서 그날 서비스되는 Main meal / Entree가 어떤 종류인지 메뉴를 정확히 숙지하는 것이 매우 중요하다.

승객이 원하는 Meal의 선택이 불가능할 경우에는 Galley 담당 승무원이나 다른 승무원에게 해당 meal이 남아있는지 확인하고, 없을 경우에는 승객에게 정중히 양해를 구한 후 다른 메뉴를 권하도록 해야 한다.

와인은 Meal Tray를 승객 테이블에 올려놓은 뒤 서비스한다. 이때 와인 종류를 간략하게 소개하고 Label이 승객에게 향하게 잡고 승객의 잔에 따르도록 한다.

Vocabulary

- a little bit of
- choice
- disappointment
- entrees
- go well
- meal
- my apologies
- recommend
- request
- return
- run out of
- set up
- tray table
- try
- upright position
- Would you mind~

Key Expression

- Would you pull out your table?
- Could you open your tray table, please?
- May I set up your tray table?
- Would you mind the opening your tray table, please?
- Would you like to open your tray table?
- We'll be serving lunch now.
- We have choice of beef or fish for lunch. Which one would you prefer?
- Would you care for some wine with your meal?
- Would you like to have red or white wine?
- I'm afraid we've run out of the steak.
- I'm sorry for the disappointment, but we are out of the beef today.
- Just a moment please and I'll see what I can do.

1) Meal Service

Dialogue 1 One choice of meal (Short flight) 1

C: Good afternoon, sir. Could you open your tray table, please?

P: Sure. What is on the menu for lunch?

C: We're serving Thai style chicken with vegetables today.

P: I don't really like chicken.
Do you have anything else?

C: I'm sorry, but I'm afraid we only have chicken on this flight.

P: Okay, I'll take it anyway.

C: I'm sorry. Here's your meal.
I hope you enjoy your meal.

P: Thank you.

C: You're welcome.

Dialogue 2 One choice of meal (Short flight) 2

C: Sir, we are serving lunch, now.
Would you like to open your tray table, please?

P: O.K.

C: Thank you. Here's your meal.
It's fish with fried rice.
Would you care for some wine?

P: Yes, please. Let me have white wine please.

C: Would you like something else to drink?

P: May I have some water?

C: Certainly sir. Here's your water.
Enjoy your meal.

Dialogue 3 Medium and Long-haul flight 1

C: Please return your seat to the upright position.
We are going to serve dinner soon. May I have your tray table?

P: Sure.

C: We have beef with rice or chicken with noodle.
Which one would you prefer?

P: Beef with rice, please.

C: Would you like to drink some wine? We have white and red wine.

P: Red wine, please.

C: Here you go. Enjoy your meal.

P: Thank you.

Dialogue 4 Medium and Long-haul flight 2

C: Ma'am, we are serving lunch, now.
Would you like to open your tray table, please?
We have beefsteak with potatoes and chicken with rice.

P: I'll have steak.

C: Here you are.
Would you care for some wine with your meal?
We have California red wine or Chilean white wine.

P: What do you recommend?

C: Red wine goes well with steak. Would you like to try it?

P: Sure.

C: Here's your red wine. Would you like something else to drink?

P: No, thanks.

C: Enjoy your meal, ma'am.

Dialogue 5 Medium and Long-haul flight 3

C: We have a choice of Chicken teriyaki or Korean style of beef.
Which one would you prefer?

P1: I'd like the chicken Teriyaki, please.

C: Certainly, ma'am.
Would you mind opening your tray table, please?
Here is your meal.
(to the next passenger P2) How about you, sir?

P2: Well, I'll try the Korean style beef.

C: Here you are.

C: (to passenger 1) Would you care for some wine?

P1: yes, please.

C: Red or white wine, ma'am?

P1: I'll have white, please.

C: Here you are.
(to passenger p2) How about you, sir?

P2: I'll have white wine too.

C: Here's your wine. Enjoy your meal.

Dialogue 6 Run out of meal choice 1

C: Excuse me ma'am.
Here are two meal option today, beefsteak and Chinese style fish.
But we don't have beefsteak anymore.
Would you like to try the fish?

P: I see. Then I'll have the fish.

C: I'm sorry, ma'am. Here you are. Would you like some wine?

P: Yes. I'll have a little bit of white wine, please.

C: Thank you for your understanding. I hope you enjoy your meal.

Dialogue 7 Run out of meal choice 2

C: Here is your meal, ma'am.

P: Excuse me. What kind of meal is this?

C: It's vegetable lasagna, ma'am.

P: I don't want to have lasagna. Do you have any beef left?

C: My apologies, but we've run out of the beef today.

P: Well I'm sorry but I'm not eating lasagna.

C: I'm terribly sorry.
Just a moment please, I'll see what I can do for you.
Would you like some bread while you are waiting?

Dialogue 8 Run out of meal choice 2

P: I'll have beefsteak.

C: I'm sorry, sir.
I'm afraid I don't have that meal anymore.
We only have chicken available.

P: I don't want chicken.

C: Give me a moment please. I'll check if there is any steak left in another galley.
(a few minutes later)
I'm very sorry, sir.
I have checked with the other crew, but we don't have any steak left.
Would you like to have chicken?
Otherwise would you care for some bread and salad instead?

Practice 10

prefer / mind / return / else / serving / tray / table / moment / what / can / instead / run / out / upright / position

1. Please ____ your seat to the ______ _______.
2. Which one would you _______?
3. Could you open your ______ _______?
4. Would you ______ opening your tray table, please?
5. We are _______ lunch now.
6. I'm afraid we've _____ ______ of the steak.
7. Just a _____ please and I will see ____ I ___ do.
8. Would you care for some bread and salad _______?
9. Would you like something ______ to drink?

2) Meal Service / Unexpected situation

Meal service시에는 다양한 상황이 발생할 수 있다. 특히 Special meal을 주문했는데 항공기에 탑재되지 않는 경우가 종종 있다.

그러므로 담당 승무원이 사전에 승객이 order한 special meal이 탑재되어 있는지를 확인하는 작업이 무엇보다 중요하며, 만일 특별 기내식이 탑재 되지 않을 경우는 대체 할 수 있는 식사를 제공할 수 있도록 최선을 다해야 한다. 무엇보다도 승객 성명과 좌석번호 등을 확인해서 승무원이 가지고 있는 Manifest(승객명단) 확인해 보고 응대할 수 있어야 하겠다.

기내식이 충분히 데워지지 않았다거나 기내식에 머리카락이나 이물질이 들어 있을 경우 등 승객이 불쾌감을 드러낼 경우는 먼저 사과하고 양해를 구한 후 신속하게 대처하도록 한다.

Tip

특별 기내식, 즉 Special Meal은 승객이 종교나 건강상의 이유, 또는 개인의 기호에 따라 항공기 탑승 전에 미리 예약해야 하는 기내식 종류로서, 전세계 항공사에서 제공하는 서비스로 그 종류도 매우 다양하다.
예를 들어, 종교식으로 유대교인을 위한 Kosher meal, 이슬람교도를 위한 Moslem meal, 힌두교도인을 위한 Hindu meal 등이 있으며, 당뇨병 환자, 심장병, 저열량, 저콜레스테롤식 등 여러 가지 건강식이 있다. 아울러, 가장 흔하게 볼 수 있는 Special meal은 바로 Child meal과 Vegetarian meal 이 되겠다. Child meal은 만 2세 이상 12세 어린이에게 제공되는 식사로 아이들이 좋아하는 샌드위치, 햄버거, 스파게티, 치킨너겟 등 여러 가지 메뉴에서 선택할 수 있고, Vegetarian meal은 채식으로 이 또한 서양식과 동양식으로 나뉘며, 우유 및 유제품이 같이 조리되었는가에 아닌가에 따라 또 나뉘게 된다. 참고로, 유아를 위한 Baby meal은 대부분의 항공사에서 비행 시 구비되어 있다고 볼 수 있다.

Vocabulary

• accept	• allergic	• assort
• delicious	• expect	• heat up

Key Expression

- I'm sorry but I'm allergic to seafood.
- I'll come back to you soon.
- I will check on your meal immediately.
- We are scheduled to land in 90 minutes.
- Could I have meal later on during the flight?
- I will heat it up for you.
- When I make my reservation~
- What type of special meal did you order?
- Your meal wasn't loaded from Seoul.
- Please accept our apologies.
- Do you have any more left?

Dialogue 1 Allergic to seafood on short flight

P: What's the meal today?

C: We have fish tempura, sir.

P: I'm sorry but I'm allergic to seafood.
Do you have anything else?

C: I'm sorry but we only offer fish on this flight.
I'll check whether we have anything else to offer you.
Would you like a drink while you are waiting?

P: No thanks.

C: All right. I'll check and get back to you.

P: Thank you.

Dialogue 2 지금 식사하고 싶지 않은 승객 1

P: I'm not really hungry right now.
Would it be possible for me to have my meal later on during the flight?

C: I'm sorry to let you know that we won't have enough time to serve you later on.
We'll be landing in about 90 minutes.

P: I see. I guess I'll eat now then.

C: Thank you for your understanding.
Here's your meal. Please enjoy.

Dialogue 3 지금 식사하고 싶지 않은 승객 2

C: Good evening, sir. We have a choice of New York steak and Chicken curry.

P: Excuse me, I'm not that hungry now.
Could I have my meal later on?

C: We're able to serve your meal later if you tell us within 1 hour.

P: O.K. Thank you.

C: Please let me know when you are ready to eat.

P: Yes, I will.

Dialogue 4 식사하고 싶지 않은 승객 3

C: We have a choice of beef or fish. Which one would you care for?

P: No, thank you. I'm not hungry.

C: Would you like some salad instead?

P: No, I'm fine.

Dialogue 5 Lukewarm Meal

P: Excuse me. I think my meal is not hot enough.

C: I'm terribly sorry, sir. I will heat that up for you immediately.
Would you like to have some bread rolls while you are waiting, sir?
(a few minutes later)
Here's your meal. I'm sorry for the inconvenience.

Dialogue 6 Special Meals 1

P: Excuse me.
When I made my reservation, I requested a low cholesterol meal.

C: I'm sorry, sir. May I have your name, please?

P: My name is Steven Kim.

C: Thank you, sir. I'll check on your meal immediately.
(a few minutes later)
Thank you for waiting, sir. We are preparing your meal now.
It'll be ready soon.
(a few minutes later)

Here is your meal. I'm sorry for the inconvenience, sir.

Enjoy your meal.

Dialogue 7 Special Meals 2

C: We have a choice of beef or chicken, which would you prefer?

P: Excuse me. When I made my reservation, I requested a special meal.

C: I'm sorry, ma'am. May I have your name, please?

What type of special meal did you order?

P: My name is Kelly Affleck. I requested a western vegetarian meal.

C: I'm sorry for the inconvenience. I'll check on your meal right away.

(after checking the passenger's special meal)

Thanks you for waiting Ms. Affleck.

We have your western vegetarian meal and we are heating it up now.

It will be ready in a few minutes.

(a few minutes later)

Here you are. Enjoy your meal, ma'am.

Dialogue 8 Special Meals 3

P: Excuse me. I requested a vegetarian meal when I made a reservation.

C: Oh, is that right? May I have your name, please?

P: Yes. I'm James Norton.

C: Thank you, sir. I'll check for you immediately.

(crew member checks the list)

I'm very sorry, sir. But your meal wasn't loaded from Seoul.

There must be some mistake. Please accept our apologies.

Instead, would you care for a vegetarian salad, sir?

Perhaps a plate of assorted fruit, cheese and vegetables?

P: That's very disappointing. Then, I guess I have no choice.

Dialogue 9 Foreign objects in the food

P: Excuse me, have a look here, how come there's a hair in my meal?
I can't eat this.

C: I'm very sorry, ma'am. I'll get you another meal right away.
(a few minutes later)
Thank you for waiting. Here's another meal.
Please accept our apologies.

P: O.K. Don't worry.

C: Is there anything else I can help you with?

P: No, I'm fine.

C: Please enjoy your meal.

Dialogue 10 Passenger requests for extra meal

P: Excuse me. This beef was delicious. Do you have any more left?

C: I'm glad you enjoyed it. Just a moment, let me check for you.
I'm sorry, but we don't have any extra meals left.
Could I get you something else instead?
Perhaps some more bread rolls?

Practice 11

requested / serve / accept / preparing / immediately / during / offer / enjoy / check / heat / reservation

1. I'm afraid we don't have enough time to ______ you.
2. Could I have my meal later on ________the flight?
3. I will check whether we have anything else to ______ for you.
4. I will _____ that up for you.
5. I'll check on your meal ____________.
6. We are __________ your meal now.
7. When I made my ______, I ______ a special meal.
8. Please ________ our apologies.
9. Let me ________ for you.
10. I hope you _______ your meal.

3) Coffee & Tea Service

승객들에게 Meal tray와 음료가 제공되고 나면 이어서 커피와 차를 서비스한다. 차와 함께 커피는 신선한 맛을 위해 서비스 직전에 Brew 하고 설탕, 크림 아울러 Lemon slice(Tea service를 위해 탑재되어 있음)와 함께 Cart 위에 준비해서 서비스하게 된다. 항공사에 따라서 Coffee pot 또는 Tea pot을 설탕, 크림을 올려놓은 Small tray와 함께 객실을 걸어다니면서 서비스하기도 한다.

참고로, Tea & Coffee service시에는 브랜디와 함께 여러 가지 식후주를 같이 제공한다. 특히, 서양문화권의 승객들은 커피와 함께 비교적 알코올 성분이 강하고 설탕이나 향료가 함유되어 있는 식후주를 많이 마시므로 그 종류도 꼭 숙지해야 한다.

Vocabulary

- glad
- great
- in a minutes
- lemon slice
- need
- tray

Key Expression

- May I offer you a cup of coffee?
- Would you care for some coffee?
- That would be nice.
- I've had enough.
- Would you care for some lemon slices with your tea?
- May I take your meal tray?
- Have you finished with your meal?
- I'm glad to hear that.
- Please take your time.

Dialogue 1 Coffee service 1

C: May I offer you a cup of coffee, sir?

P: Yes, please.

C: May I have your cup, please? Thank you, sir.
Here is your coffee, sir.

P: I need some cream and sugar.

C: They are on your meal tray, sir.
If you need some extra sugar or cream, just let me know.

Dialogue 2 Coffee service 2

C: Would you care for some coffee?

P: Yes. Please

C: May I have your cup, please? Thank you.
Here's your coffee.

P: Can I have some sugar?

C: Sure. Here you are. Would you like some brandy?

P: No. I'm find. Do you have Irish cream, instead?

Dialogue 3 Coffee Refill

C: Would you care for some more coffee, sir?

P1: Yes, please.

C: May I have your cup, please?
Thank you. Here you are, sir.
(to P2) How about you sir? Would you like some more coffee?

P2: No, Thanks. I've had enough.

Dialogue 4 Tea service 1

C1: Would you like some coffee, sir?

P: Well··· I want to have some tea, please.

C1: Certainly, sir. Another attendant will serve you tea in a minute.
(a moment later)

C2: Would you care for some tea, sir?

P: Yes, please.

C2: May I have your cup, please? Thank you.
Would you care for some lemon slices with your tea?

P: That would be nice.

C2: Here is your tea, Enjoy your drink, sir.

Dialogue 5 Tea service 2

C: Would you like to have some tea?

P: What kind of tea do you have?

C: We have black tea or green tea, ma'am.

P: Oh, I like green tea. May I have green tea?

C: Certainly. Be careful it's hot.

Dialogue 6 Tea Refill

C: Would you care for some more tea?

P: Yes, please.

C: May I have your cup, please?

Thank you. Here you are.

P: Can I have lemon slices?

C: Sure. Enjoy your drink.

4) Collection of meal tray

승객식사가 대부분 끝났을 때 Meal tray 회수를 시작하며, 식사를 먼저 제공받았던 승객부터 service를 했던 flow에 맞게 collection하면 된다. 이때 회수해도 되는지 승객에게 허락을 받는 후 tray를 회수해서 cart 안에 넣도록 한다.

아울러, Tray 회수 시 음료나 물을 찾는 승객들이 많으므로 cart 위에 준비해서 나가도록 한다.

Dialogue 1 Meal tray collection 1

C: May I take your meal tray, sir?

P: Sure.

C: I hope you enjoyed your meal.

P: Of course, I enjoyed it.

C: I'm glad to hear that.

Dialogue 2 Meal tray collection 2

C: Have you finished your meal?

P: Yes, I have.

C: May I take your meal tray?

P: Yes, please.

C: How was your meal?

P: It was great.

C: I'm glad you enjoyed it.

Dialogue 3 Passenger is not finished the meal

C: May I take your meal tray, sir?

P: No, I'm not finished, yet.

C: I'm sorry, sir.

Please take your time and enjoy your meal.

Practice 12

meal / take / tray / hear / enough / have / need / would / serve

1. May I ______ your cup, please?
2. I _______ some cream and sugar.
3. No thanks. I've had ________.
4. That _________be nice.
5. Another attendant will ________ you tea in a minute.
6. May I take your_______ ________?
7. I'm glad to _______ that.
8. Please ______ your time and enjoy your meal.

4. In-flight entertainment

Meal service가 끝나고 나면 승객들은 Entertainment service를 이용할 수 있게 된다. 물론 개인용 비디오가 장착되어 있는 항공기를 이용하는 승객들은 따로 시간이나 시점에 구애받지 않고, 항공기 이륙 후 Entertainment system이 작동될 때부터 여러 가지 단편물, 뉴스, 드라마, 영화 등 다양한 영상물과 다양한 종류의 음악, 그리고 게임들도 즐길 수 있다.

개인용 비디오가 장착되지 않은 항공기의 경우 승객들이 언제, 어떤 영화를 시청할 수 있는지 문의하는 경우가 있으므로, 사전에 기내에서 상영될 영화제목을 꼭 체크하고 비행에 임하도록 한다.

최근에는 항공사마다 개인용 모니터를 장착한 기종이 많으므로 개인용 비디오 장비의 이용방법에 대한 질문도 많이 받게 된다. 이때 승객들에게 사용법을 정확히 전달해 줄 수 있도록 사용법을 숙지하는 것도 매우 중요하다.

요즘 외국항공사 특히 저비용 항공사들은 비행기티켓 가격을 저렴하게 제공하기 위해 Earphone을 판매하는 경우도 있다. 아울러 Earphone/Headset이 고장이거나 좌석에 문제가 있어 Earphone/Headset을 사용하지 못할 경우 어떻게 응대해야 할지 참고해 보도록 하자.

Vocabulary

- available
- be going to
- be willing to
- bother
- channel selector
- earphone jack
- empty
- firmly
- in-flight
- locate
- magazine
- move
- occupied
- program
- right after
- seat pocket
- show
- volume control

Key Expression

- What kind of music is available?
- What kind of music do you have?
- We have pop, rock, jazz and classical music.
- When are you showing the movie?
- The movie will be shown in about ~
- The movie will be started~
- What movie are you showing today?
- We are going to show~
- This earphone is out of order.
- Let me get you another earphones.
- I'll see if there are any empty seats available~
- I'm afraid that all the seats are occupied.

1) Music Information

Dialogue 1 Music information 1

P: What kind of music do you have?

C: Well, we have pop, rock, jazz and classical music.
This entertainment guide will show you today's in-flight music program.

Dialogue 2 Music information 2

P: Excuse me. What kind of music is available?

C: We have pop, rock, jazz and classical music.
There is more information about our music in your in-flight entertainment magazine, located in your seat pocket.
Here's our music program. Enjoy the flight.

2) Movie program Information

Dialogue 1 Movie program information 1

P: What movie are you showing today?

C: We are going to show "Les Miserable"
For more information, please refer to the entertainment guide in your seat pocket.

P: Oh, I see. Thanks.

C: You're welcome, sir. Enjoy the movie.

Dialogue 2 Movie program information 2

P: When are you showing the movie today?

C: The movie will be shown right after the meal, sir.

P: When will that be?

C: It will start in about 30 minutes.

P: What's the title of the movie?

C: It will be "Jack Reacher" starring Tom Cruise.

P: Can I get a headset for the movie?

C: Yes, but we charge for a headset. It's 5 dollars.

P: Here's 5 dollars. What channel is the movie on?

C: Channel 2, sir. Enjoy your movie.

Dialogue 3 Movie timing

P: When are you showing the movie today?

C: The movie will begin right after the meal service, in about two and a half hours.

P: Thanks.

C: You're welcome.

3) Problem with Entertainment System

Dialogue 1 Earphone out of order 1

P: Excuse me. I think, my earphones are not working.

C: Let me check them, sir.

(after checking volume control, channel selector, and whether earphone jack is firmly in place)

Can you hear anything now?

P: Now they're working. Thank you.

C: You're welcome.

Dialogue 2 Earphone out of order 2

P: Excuse me. I think my earphones are not working.

C: Excuse me, sir. Let me check it. Can you hear it, now?

P: No, I can't hear anything.

C: Just a moment, please. Let me get you another set.

(bring the new ones)

Are they working?

P: Yes, they are working. Thank you.

C: My pleasure.

Dialogue 3 Earphone out of order 3

P: My headphones aren't working.

C: Let me check them for you, sir.

Can you hear anything now?

P: No, I still can't hear anything.

C: I'll get you some new headphones right away.

(bring new ones)

Please try these headphones. Are they working?

P: No, they're not.

C: Maybe there is a problem with the seat.

I'll see if there are any empty seats available. Just a moment, please.

Dialogue 4 Passenger changes the seat due to unserviceable earphones

P: Excuse me. This earphone set is out of order.

C: Excuse me, sir. Can your hear them now?

P: No, still nothing at all.

C: I don't know what's wrong with them. Just a moment, please.

(Flight Attendant gets a new set of earphones and checks a nearby empty seat's music system)

Would you like to move to this seat over here, sir?

The sound system in this seat is working better.

P: O.K. Thank you.

Dialogue 5 Passenger changes the seat due to unserviceable entertainment system 1

P1: Excuse me. This earphone set is out of order.

C: Let me check, please. Can you hear it now?

P1: No, still nothing at all.

C: Just a moment, please. I'll see what I can do.

I'm sorry, but I'm afraid that all the seats are occupied.

Would you care for a newspaper or magazine?

P1: No, thanks. Is there any way to listen to music?

C: Wait a second, please. I'll check for you.

〈To P2〉

C: (Checking a passenger who is not using the entertainment system)
Excuse me. I'm sorry to bother you.
Will you be listening to music, ma'am?

P2: No, I'll be reading most of the time. Why?

C: We have a passenger right over there who would like to listen to music,
But the sound system in her seat is out of order.
If you don't mind could you change seats with her?

P2: Sure. No problem.

C: Thank you very much. Come this way, please.

〈To P1〉

C: Excuse me. This gentleman is willing to change seats with you.
This way, please.

P1: Oh, Thank you.

P2: No problem.

〈To P2〉

C: Thank you for your concern. Is there anything I can get for you?

P2: That's all right.

C: Thank you again. I hope you enjoy the flight.

Dialogue 6 Passenger changes the seat due to unserviceable entertainment system 2 (No empty seat)

P: Excuse me. I think my earphone set is not working.

C: Oh is that right? Let me check your earphones. Can you hear it now?

P: No, still nothing at all.

C: Just a moment, please. I'll see what I can do.
I'm sorry, but I'm afraid that all the seats are occupied.

P: Oh, that's O.K. Don't worry.

C: I'm sorry, sir. May I get you a newspaper?

P: No, thanks.

C: If you need anything during the flight, please let me know.

Practice 13

occupied / after / kind / hear / bother / right / order / willing

1. What _______ of music do you have?
2. The movie will be shown _______ _______ the meal service.
3. I think my earphone set is out of ________.
4. Can you ________ it now?
5. I'm sorry to _________ you.
6. This gentleman is __________ to change seats with you.
7. I'm afraid that all the seats are ___________.

4) Cabin preparation for movie.

영화 상영 시에는 보다 나은 화면을 위해, 또는 쉬고자 하는 승객을 위해 기내 객실 등이 어둡게 조절된다. 따라서 창문덮개가 Open되어 있을 때에는 정중히 상황설명을 하고 닫을 수 있도록 한다. 아울러, 독서 등의 사용법과 기타 장비의 사용법을 잘 모르는 승객에게는 친절하게 설명해 드리도록 한다.

Vocabulary

- button
- closing
- go ahead
- hesitate
- push
- reading light

Key Expression

- Would you mind closing your window shade, please?
- May I close the window shade for the movie?
- We will be showing the movie shortly.
- Would you like me to turn on the reading light?
- Please push the reading light button.
- Would you come this way?
- Please don't hesitate to call us if you need anything.

Dialogue 1 영화 상영 준비 1

C: Excuse me, sir. Would you mind closing your window shade, please?
We will be showing the movie shortly.

P: No, I don't mind. Please go ahead.

C: Thank you, sir. Please, enjoy the movie.

Dialogue 2 영화 상영 준비 2

C: Excuse me, ma'am. We will be playing a movie shortly.
May I close the window shade for the movie?

P: No, I won't watch the movie and I don't want to be in darkness.

C: I understand. However, it is for other passengers to have a better view of the movie. After the movie, you may open it later.

P: O.K.

C: Thank you for your cooperation.
Please don't hesitate to call us if you need anything.

Dialogue 3 Bulkhead passengers at movie time

C: Excuse me, ma'am. Are you going to watch the movie?

P: Yes, I am.

C: I'm afraid you won't be able to see the screen very well from this seat. Would you like to change seats? We have some empty seats in the middle of the cabin.

P: Oh, that sounds good.

C: Then, would you come this way?
Here is your seat. Enjoy the movie.

P: Thank you.

Dialogue 4 Using reading light 1

C: Excuse me, ma'am. We'll be showing the movie soon.
Would you mind if I close the shade, please?

P: I'm not going to watch the movie. I'm going to read, instead.

C: Certainly, ma'am.
But I'm afraid we have to close the window shades while the movie is showing.
Would you like me to turn on the reading light for you?
Thank you. Would you care for something to drink?

P: No, thank you.

C: Please enjoy the flight, ma'am.

Dialogue 5 Using reading light 2

C: Excuse me. We'll be showing the movie shortly.
Would you mind closing your window shade, please?

P: I'm not going to watch the movie.

C: I'm sorry to let you know, but we need to close the window shades while the movie is showing.
May I help you to turn on the reading light?

P: No, thanks. I'll do by myself. Where is it?

C: Please press the reading light button which is located in your armrest.
May I offer you something to drink, sir?

P: No, thank you.

C: Thank you for your concern.

Practice 14

come / turn / on / closing / press / hesitate

1. Would you mind __________ your window shades, please?
2. Don't ___________ to call me if you need anything.
3. Would you like me to _______ ______the reading light?
4. Please _______the reading light button.
5. Would you ________ this way?

5. In-flight sales

기내 면세품 판매는 각 항공사에서 제공하는 중요한 기내서비스 중의 하나이다.

각 항공사들은 국제선 항공편에서 승객의 편의를 위해 다양한 면세상품(화장품, 주류, 담배, 기념품 등)을 판매하고 있다. 또한 기내주문, 사전예약 주문, 귀국편 예약 주문제도 등을 통해 승객이 더욱 편리하게 이용할 수 있도록 하고 있다.

면세품 판매 시 승무원은 도착지 해당국가의 면세 허용기준을 꼭 숙지하여 승객이 문의 할 경우 올바른 정보를 제공해야 한다.

Vocabulary

- allow
- allowance
- bring
- change
- correct
- currency
- duty free
- item
- liter
- purchase
- refund
- sell
- sold out
- souvenir
- unacceptable
- unavailable

Key Expression

- Would you like to purchase any duty-free items?
- Would you like to buy any duty-free items?
- I'm afraid I don't have change right now.
- I will bring your change as soon as I can.
- We can only give a refund on items purchased during the flight.
- Is that correct?
- I'm afraid it has sold out.
- We are not able to sell duty-free items, because we are preparing to land.

Dialogue 1 In-flight sales 1

C: Excuse me. Would you like to purchase any In-flight duty-free items?

P: No, thank.

C: If you need something, you may refer to the in-flight sales magazine in your seat pocket.

P: Thank you.

Dialogue 2 In-flight Sales 2

C: Would you like to buy any duty-free items?

P: What kind of items do you have?

C: We have liquors, cigarette, cosmetics, perfumes and some souvenir items. What would you like to buy?

P: I need a bottle of whiskey.
Do you know how much whiskey I can take into Bangkok?

C: You're allowed one liter of liquor.

P: Okay. Bring me a bottle of whiskey.

C: Certainly, sir.
What kind of whiskey would you care for?
We have Jonnie Walker Blue, Ballantine and Royal Salute.

P: A bottle of Royal Salute, please.

C: How would you like to pay? We accept Korean Won, US dollars, Yen, and Euro.

P: Do you take credit card?

C: Of course you can pay with that. It is 150 US dollar, sir.

P: Here you are.

C: Could I have your signature, please?

Dialogue 3 In-flight Sales 3

P: How much is the Chanel perfume?

C: It's forty US dollars, sir.

P: Can I pay in Euro?

C: Certainly.

P: How much is it in Euro?

C: It is 30 Euro, sir.

P: By the way, can you recommend me any gift items?

P: We have so many of them, however is it for a lady or a gentleman?

P: It's for my son. He is 15 years old.

C: Oh, then, would you like to have a look at these pens?

Dialogue 4 면세품 종류

C: May I take your order for any duty-free items, sir?

P: Yes, What do you have?

C: We have alcohol, souvenirs, cosmetics, cigarettes and perfumes for sale. This shopping guide will give you information about our in-flight sales items, sir.

Dialogue 5 Duty-free allowance

P: Excuse me. Do you know how much duty-free I'm allowed to I bring into Korea?

C: You can bring one bottle of alcohol, 60ml of perfume and 200 pieces of cigarettes. Also you are allowed to bring less than 400US dollars of goods for personal use and gifts. For more information please refer to the customs form.

P: Oh, I see. Thanks.

C: You're welcome.

Dialogue 6 Change available

C: Excuse me. Would you like to buy any duty-free items, sir?

P: Could I have two cartons of Marlboro and a bottle of Chivas Regal?

C: Certainly, sir. Here you are. That will be 40 US dollars.

P: Here's 50 dollars.

C: Thank you, sir.
Here is your change, 10 dollars.

Dialogue 7 Change unavailable

P: Excuse me. I have to buy chocolate, but all I have is a 100 dollar bill. Do you have change?

C: I'm sorry, but I'm afraid I don't have change right now.
But I will bring you your change as soon as I can.
Would that be all right, sir?

P: No problem. Let me have the chocolate.

C: Certainly. It is 25 dollars. Wait for me, please.
(write down the seat number, the amount received, cost of item and name)
(a few minutes later)
Thank you for waiting, sir.
Here's your change, 75 dollars. Is that correct, sir?

P: Yes, it's correct. Thanks.

C: My pleasure.

Dialogue 8 Passenger waiting for change 1

P: Excuse me. Where's my change?

C: Thank you for waiting, ma'am.
Here's your change, 20 dollars. Is that correct?

P: Thank you.

Dialogue 9 Passenger waiting for change 2

P: Excuse me. Where's my change?

C: I'm sorry. I still don't have change yet.
I'll bring you your change as soon as possible, sir.

Dialogue 10 Unacceptable currency

P: Excuse me. Do you accept Malaysian Ringgit?

C: I'm sorry, but I'm afraid we do not accept ringgit, ma'am.
We only accept U.S. dollars, Korean won, Euro and Japanese Yen.

Dialogue 11 Refund

P: Excuse me. Can I get a refund on this perfume?

C: May I ask where you bought it, ma'am?

P: I bought it just now, about 10 minutes ago.

C: Certainly, ma'am. Just a moment, please.
May I have the perfume?
(a few minutes later)
Here's your refund, ma'am.

Dialogue 12 Refund not available

P: Excuse me. Is it possible to get a refund on these cosmetics?

C: Could you tell me where you bought them, sir?

P: I bought them at the airport duty-free shop.

C: I'm sorry, but I'm afraid we can only give refunds for items purchased during the flight, sir.

P: I see. Thank you.

Dialogue 13 Items is sold out or no stock 1

P: Excuse me. I'd like to buy a bottle of Camus, please.

C: I'm sorry, ma'am, but I'm afraid it has sold out.
Would you care for a bottle of Scotch whisky, instead?

P: Yes, please.

C: Certainly. That will be 70dollars. Thank you.

Dialogue 14 Items is sold out or no stock 2

P: Excuse me. I'd like to buy a bottle of Jonnie Walker Blue, please?

C: I'm sorry, sir but I'm afraid it has sold out.
Would you like a bottle of Ballantine, instead?

P: No, thanks.

C: O.K. Have a nice flight.

Dialogue 15 Passenger requests sale item before cart reaches their aisle

P: I'd like to buy a bottle of perfume, please.

C: Certainly. But, would you please wait till we bring the cart to your seat, ma'am? I'll serve you as fast as I can. Thank you.

Dialogue 16 Duty free items request before landing

P: Excuse me. I'd like to buy some duty-free items.

C: Oh, I'm sorry sir. We are not able to sell duty-free items, because we are preparing to land.

P: Oh, I see.

C: Thank you for your understanding.

Practice 15

bring / preparing / allowed / purchase / signature / sold / out / change / would

1. Would you like to ________ any duty-free items?
2. You are ________ one liter of liquor.
3. Could I have your ________, please?
4. I will ________ your change as soon as I can.
5. Here is your ________.
6. I'm afraid it has ______ ______.
7. We are not able to sell duty-free items, because we are ________ to land.

6. C.I.Q

객실 승무원은 승객의 입국 편의를 위해 항공기가 목적지에 도착하기 전 해당 국가에서 요구하는 입국서류를 승객에게 배포해야 하며, 또한 작성에 어려움을 겪는 승객에게 도움을 줄 수 있어야 한다.

C.I.Q 서류는 항공사와 항공기 노선에 따라 승객에게 배포하는 시점이 조금씩 다를 수 있으나 이륙 후 제공하는 것을 원칙으로 한다. 승무원은 도착지 국가에서 필요로 하는 서류의 종류를 정확하게 숙지해서 승객에게 안내 시 차질이 없도록 한다.

특히 세관신고서는 허위작성 시 법적으로 처벌을 받을 수 있으므로 승객이 정확히 작성할 수 있도록 안내하는 것이 중요하며, 면세 허용량에 대한 정보도 같이 제공하는 것이 좋다.

Tip C.I.Q 란

C-Customs(세관), I-Immigration(출입국관리), Qarantine(검역)의 약칭으로 목적지 출입국 때 거치는 수속이다.

Vocabulary

- arrival card
- customs declaration form
- exit
- overnight
- staying
- citizen
- declare
- health questionnaire
- resident
- transit
- continue
- disembarkation card
- immigrant
- sightseeing

Key Expression

- Do I need to fill out this card?
- Would you like me help you with it?
- Are you a resident?
- You don't need to fill out the card.
- Will you be leaving the transit area at the airport?
- All passengers must fill out both sides of the card.
- Would you like me to help you with it?
- Are you staying in Korea?

Dialogue 1 Disembarkation card

P: Excuse me. I'm going to stay in Korea for three weeks.
Do I need to fill out disembarkation card?

C: Yes, ma'am. Foreigners entering Korea must fill out the disembarkation card.
May I help you fill it out?

P: No, thanks.

Dialogue 2 Disembarkation card - Resident

P: Excuse me. When I left Korea, they put this ED card(=embarkation card) in my passport. Do I have to fill it out again?

C: Are you a resident?

P: Yes, I am.

C: Please just fill in your flight number and the place of departure.

Dialogue 3 Disembarkation card - Tourist

P: Excuse me. I'll be staying in Korea for one week.
Do I need to fill out this card?

C: Yes, sir. All foreign passengers entering Korea must fill out the arrival card.
Would you like me to help you with it, sir?

P: Yes, please.

Dialogue 4 Transit passengers 1

C: Excuse me. These are the entry cards for Korea.

P: I'll be at Incheon only for a few hours. Do I need this card?

C: Will you be leaving the transit area at the airport?

P: No, I'll be at the airport and then I'll be flying on to Shanghai.

C: No, sir. You don't need to fill out the card.

P: Thank you.

Dialogue 5 Transit Passengers 2

P: I'm going to meet my friend in Seoul this afternoon.
And I will continue flight this evening to Sydney.
Do I need this card?

C: Yes, you do, ma'am.
Please fill out the card and write "Transit" here.

Dialogue 6 In transit Passenger 3

C: Are you visiting Korea?

P: No, I won't. My next flight leaves just 2 hours after landing.

C: Then you don't need to fill out any entry documents.

Dialogue 7 Customs Declaration card - Resident and Tourist

P: Excuse me. Do I need this card for Korea?

C: All passengers must fill out both sides of the customs declaration card.
Would you like me to help you with the card, sir?

P: No, thanks.

C: All right.

Dialogue 8 Passenger is given the wrong version card

P: Excuse me. What kind of card is this?

C: Oh, I'm sorry, ma'am. I'll get you the English version one.
Just a moment, please. Here you are, ma'am.
Shall I help you with it?

Dialogue 9 Entering Korea

C: Are you staying in Korea?

P: Yes, I'll be in Korea for three weeks.

F: Then, please fill out this arrival card, customs declaration form and health questionnaire.

Dialogue 10 | Entering US-Tourist

P: Excuse me. Do I have to fill this out?

C: Are you a U.S. citizen or a resident, ma'am?

P: No, I'm not.

C: Then, you need to fill out this immigration card and customs declaration form.

Would you like me to help you?

P: No, that's O.K.

C: All right, ma'am. Have a nice trip.

Dialogue 11 | Entering US-Immigrant

P: Excuse me. I live in the USA, but I'm not a citizen yet.

Do I need to fill these cards out?

C: May I ask whether you have an immigrant visa, sir?

P: Yes, I have an immigrant visa.

C: Then you only have to fill out the customs declaration form, sir.

P: Thank you.

Practice 16

version / staying / fill / out / need / leaving / like

1. Do I need to _____ _____ this card?
2. Would you _____ me to help you with it?
3. You don't _____ to fill out the card.
4. Will you be _____ the transit area?
5. I'll get you the English _____ one.
6. I will be _____ in Korea.

7. Destination Information

1) Flight information

항공기가 이륙 후, 해당 항공기의 기장은 방송을 통해 항공기 운항 정보와 비행시간, 현지 도착시간이나 날씨 등 전반적인 목적지 정보를 제공한다.

하지만 비행 중 이를 듣지 못한 승객들이 현지 시간이나 시차, 날씨 등에 관한 질문을 많이 하는 관계로, 승무원은 목적지의 운항 정보 및 도착지에 관한 정보를 꼭 숙지하고 있어야 한다.

Vocabulary

- ahead
- arrive
- behind
- between
- difference
- local time

Key Expression

- May I help you?
- What time is it in New York?
- Is it Monday or Sunday?
- What time are we arriving in Paris?
- We are scheduled to arrive at 2:30pm.
- Have a pleasant flight.
- Is there any time difference between Seoul and Taipei?
- Seoul is one hour ahead of Taipei.
- How long does it going to take us to get to San Francisco?
- Our scheduled flight time after take off will be 13hours.

Dialogue 1 Local time

P: Excuse me.

C: Yes? May I help you?

P: What time is it in Paris?

C: It's about 11 o'clock in the morning. Paris is 7 hours behind Seoul.

P: Oh, thanks. Is it Friday or Saturday?

C: It's Saturday.

P: What time are we arriving in Paris?

C: We are scheduled to arrive at 5:30pm, sir.

P: Thank you very much.

C: You are welcome. Have a pleasant flight, sir.

Dialogue 2 Time difference

P: Is there any time difference between Seoul and Taipei?

C: Seoul is one hour ahead of Taipei.

P: How about between Seoul and Tokyo?

C: There's no time difference between them.

Dialogue 3 Flight time

P: How long does it take to San Francisco?

C: Our scheduled flight time after take-off will be 12 hours, ma'am.

P: What's the time difference between Seoul and San Francisco?

C: San Francisco is 17 hours behind Seoul, ma'am.

P: I see. Thank you.

C: You're welcome.

Practice 17

Ahead / about / is / between / difference / may

1. ______ I help you?
2. ___ it Friday or Saturday?
3. It's _______ 10 o'clock in the morning.
4. Is there any time ________ _______ Seoul and Tokyo?
5. Seoul is one hour __________ of Taipei.

2) Destination Information

한국을 처음 방문하는 외국인 승객들은 호텔에 관한 정보나 공항에서 서울 시내로 이동하는 교통수단 등에 관련한 질문을 자주 한다.

승무원이 알고 있는 호텔정보를 제공하는 것과 더불어, 구체적인 호텔정보는 공항 내 Hotel information desk에서 자세히 안내받을 수 있다고 안내하도록 한다.

또한 시내로의 교통수단으로 공항 리무진버스, 택시 또는 공항 철도 등을 이용할 수 있다고 알려주고, 이 또한 변경사항이 있을 수 있으니 공항 내 Information desk를 이용하도록 응대한다.

아울러, 외국인 승객들은 한국인 승무원에게 서울시내에 관광하기 좋은 곳을 추천해 달라고 할 때에는 승객이 가고자 하는 목적에 맞게 추천할 수 있도록 주요 관광지에 대한 정보를 사전에 숙지하면 도움이 되며, 한국을 알리는 마음으로 정확한 정보를 제공할 수 있도록 한다.

Vocabulary

- accommodation
- cheap
- cost
- deluxe
- depending on
- district
- downtown
- exchange
- inexpensive
- rate
- recommend
- traditional
- traffic
- transportation
- various

Key Expression

- What kind of transportation is available from Incheon airport to downtown?
- It takes about one hour by limousine bus, depending on the traffic.
- How long does it take to downtown Seoul from the airport?
- Do you know any good places for shopping in Seoul?
- Could you recommend any hotels in Seoul?
- Can you tell me the exchange rate for dollars?

Dialogue 1 Transportation to Seoul-Downtown 1

P: Excuse me. It is my first trip to Korea.
What kind of transportation is available from Incheon airport to downtown, Seoul?

C: Well, we have buses, taxies and trains.
A taxi will cost about fifty thousand won depending on the traffic.
However, I'd like to recommend you to take trains because it is faster and cheaper.

P: Thank you.

C: You're welcome. Have a good time in Seoul.

Dialogue 2 Transportation to Seoul-Downtown 2

P: What's the arrival time in Seoul?

C: It's 7:20 in the morning, sir.

P: How long does it take to downtown Seoul from the airport?

C: It takes about forty minutes by taxi, but it depends on the traffic.
There are two kinds of taxis, the regular and deluxe.

P: Is there a bus service available?

C: Of course there is. There is an airport limousine bus which comes every

15 minutes.

It takes about one hour to get to downtown.

P: Thank you.

C: You're welcome. Have a nice stay in Korea.

Dialogue 3 Hotel Information

P: Excuse me. I could not book the hotel before I came to Seoul.

Can you recommend me any hotels in Seoul?

This is my first trip to Korea and I don't really know any places to stay.

C: Well… I would recommend the Hilton Hotel. It is very nice Hotel but expensive.

For a cheaper hotel, I would like to recommend Ibiza Hotel in MyungDong.

It's located in the MyungDong shopping district.

But for more information, please go to the hotel information desk on the first floor at the airport.

They'll definitely help you find good accommodations.

Have a nice stay in Korea, sir.

P: Thank you.

Dialogue 4 Shopping Information

P: Excuse me. Do you know any good places for shopping in Seoul?

C: I would recommend Itaewon.

You can get various souvenirs, inexpensive clothes, and shoes.

Also, People who work there can speak English.

P: I see. What else would you recommend for me?

C: Namdaemun Market is another place you can enjoy shopping.

It is one of the traditional markets in Korea.

The items are cheap and nice. You can get everything down there.
If you have time, you might want to go to Insadong too.
It is one of the best place for shopping and Korean cuisine.

P: Thank you.

C: My pleasure. Have a good time in Seoul.

Dialogue 5 Exchange Rate information

P: Excuse me. Can you tell me the exchange rate for dollars?

C: Well. I am not sure, but today's rate is about 1100 won to one US dollar.

P: Thank you.

C: You're welcome. Please enjoy staying in Korea.

Practice 18

how / long / takes / about / exchange / rate / transportation / available / recommend

1. What kind of ____________is ______ form Incheon airport to downtown?
2. It _____ _____ one hour by bus, depending on the traffic.
3. _____ _____ does it take to downtown Seoul from the airport?
4. Could you ________________ any hotels in Seoul?
5. Can you tell me the _________ ______ for US dollars?

Part. 05

Landing & Deplane

1. Prepare for landing
2. Disembarkation

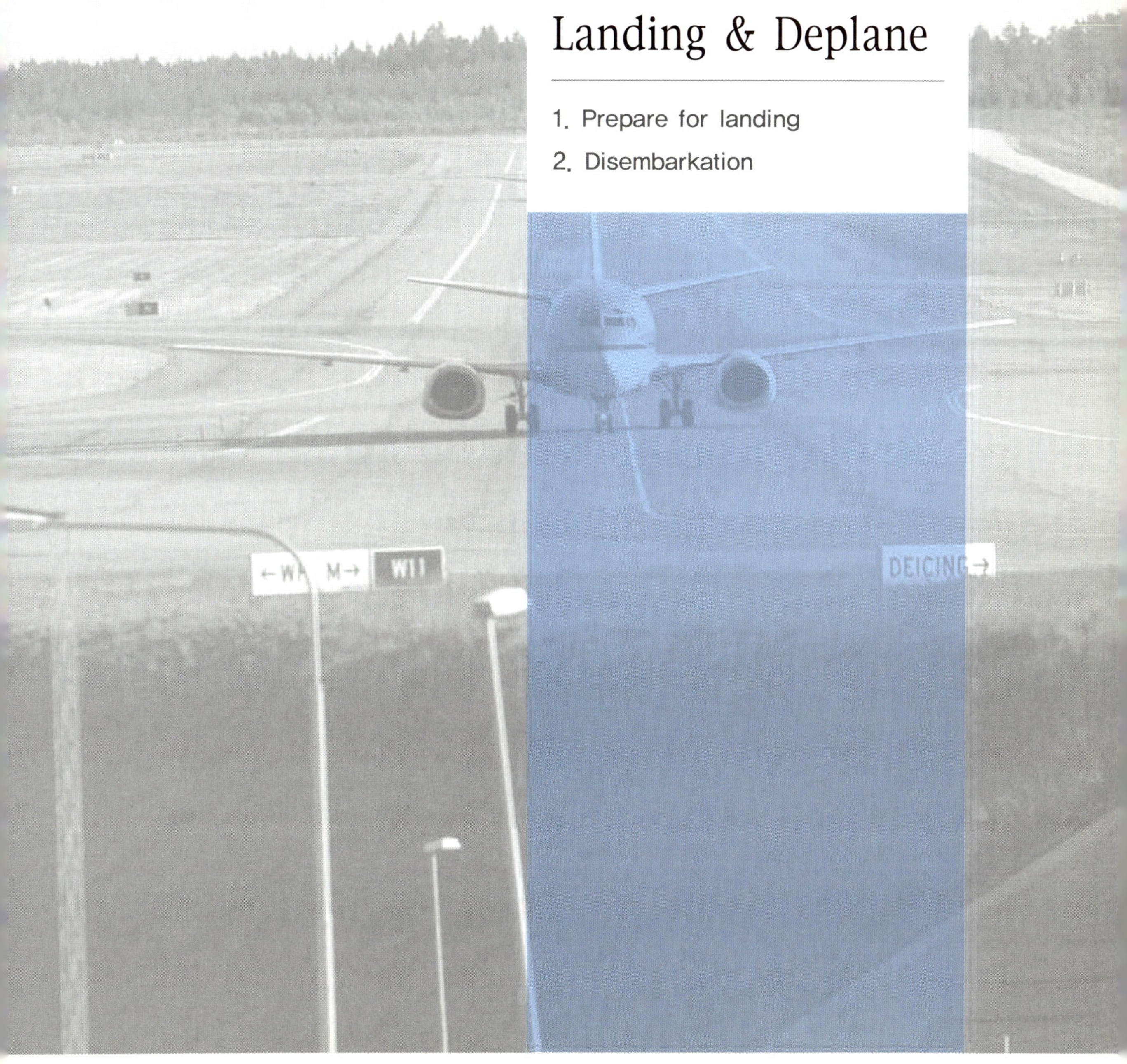

Landing & Deplane

항공기 이륙 때와 달리 착륙할 시점에는 대부분의 손님들은 제한된 공간에서 오랜 비행을 한 후이기 때문에 매우 지쳐있다고 할 수 있다. 또한 오랜 비행으로 손님들은 몸의 피곤함과, 때때로 소화불량 문제를 겪기도 한다.

비행기가 천천히 하강할 때에는 승무원들은 손님들에게 다시 한 번 안전벨트 착용, 좌석 등 받침의 원위치로 돌려놓기와 tray table을 원위치로 고정시키도록 안내한다.

통로와 비상구를 착륙에 대비 깨끗하게 정리하고, 짐들도 수화물 칸이나 좌석 밑에 보관하도록 한다.

비행기가 완전히 착륙한 후에는 손님들이 비행기가 터미널에 도착하여 좌석벨트 사인이 꺼질 때까지 좌석에서 일어나지 않도록 하며, 비행기에서 하기 하시는 손님들에게 모든 승무원들이 작별인사를 한다.

착륙 준비 업무는 다음과 같다.

▶ 착륙 전 기장 도착 안내방송 후

1) Headphone 회수 및 정위치 보관
2) 기내도서, 잡지 회수 및 보관 및 빈 컵 회수 등
3) 입국서류 작성 재확인
4) 승객의 코트 및 보관해 두었던 짐 돌려드리기

▶ 착륙 전 최종 안전점검

1) 승객의 착석, 좌석벨트 착용 상태, 좌석 등받이 및 Tray table 정위치, Arm rest 정위치
2) 승객 휴대 수화물 고정

3) 전자기기 사용금지 안내 및 Galley내 탑재물품 및 Cart 고정

4) 화장실 점검 및 승객 사용여부

Vocabulary

- comfortable
- comments
- deplane
- descend
- earphone
- fall out
- fasten
- hold
- improve
- landing
- might
- outside
- recline
- refrain
- safer

Key Expression

- How was your flight?
- We'll be landing shortly.
- Would you mind fastening your seat belt, please.
- Would you mind returning your seat to the upright position for landing.
- Here is your coat/bag, sir.
- May I have your earphones, please?
- Thank you for flying with us today.
- Thank you I hope to see you again, soon.
- Thank you for being with us today.

1. Prepare for landing

1) Collection of Headphones & Cups

Dialogue 1 헤드폰 수거 1

C: Excuse me, sir. May I have your earphone set, please?
We'll be landing shortly.

P: Here it is.

C: Thank you, sir. Did you have a nice flight, sir?

P: Yes, I did.

C: I'm glad to hear that. I hope you have a nice stay in Shanghai.

P: Thank you.

Dialogue 2 헤드폰 수거 2

C: Excuse me. May I have your earphone set, please?

We'll be landing shortly.

Thank you, sir. How was your flight?

P: Good. Thank you.

Dialogue 3 컵 수거 1

C: Excuse me, ma'am. Have you finished your drink?

P: Yes, I have.

C: Thank you, ma'am.

We'll be landing shortly. Would you mind fastening your seatbelt and closing your tray table?

Dialogue 4 컵 수거 2

C: Excuse me, sir. May I take your glass?

P: Yes, please.

C: (taking cup away) Thank you, sir.

We'll be landing shortly.

Please check your seatbelt and close your tray table.

P: Sure.

C: Thank you, sir.

2) Seatbelt, Seat back & Tray table

Dialogue 1 안전벨트 1

C: Excuse me, sir. Would you mind fastening your seatbelt, please?
We'll be landing soon. Thank you, sir.

Dialogue 2 안전벨트 2

C: Excuse me, ma'am.
Would you mind fastening your seat belt, please?
We'll be landing shortly

P: O.K.

C: Thank you.

Dialogue 3 유아 동반 보호자의 안전벨트

C: Excuse me, ma'am. Please hold your baby outside of the seatbelt, It will be safer and more comfortable.

P: Oh, I see. Thanks.

C: My pleasure. Did you have a nice flight?

Dialogue 4 좌석 등받침과 테이블

C: Excuse me, ma'am. Would you mind returning your seat back to the upright position and closing your tray table, please? We'll be landing soon.

P: Alright.

C: Thank you, ma'am. Did you enjoy the flight?

P: Yes, I did.

C: I'm happy to hear that.

3) Storage of passenger's Baggage

Dialogue 1 짐 보관 1

C: Excuse me, ma'am. Would you mind keeping your bag under your seat, please?
It might fall out during landing. Thank you.

Dialogue 2 짐 보관 2

C: Excuse me. Is this bag yours?
P: Yes, why?
F: Would you mind keeping your bag under your seat, please?
We must keep the aisle clear, ma'am.
We'll be landing shortly.

Dialogue 3 짐 보관 3

C: Excuse me. Would you mind keeping your bag under your seat in front of you, please?
It might fall out during landing.
P: O.K.
C: Thank you.

4) Returning Passenger's Clothing / Bag

Dialogue 1 승객의 짐 돌려주기 1

C: Excuse me, ma'am. Here's your coat and bag.
We'll be landing in about 10minutes.

P: Thank you.

C: You're welcome. Have a nice stay in Paris.

Dialogue 2 승객의 짐 돌려주기 2

C: Excuse me, sir. This is your suitcase, isn't it?
We'll be landing in about 10minutes.

P: Yes, thank you.

C: My pleasure. I hope you enjoyed our flight today.

Dialogue 3 승객의 짐 돌려주기 3

P: Excuse me. Would you bring me my coat?

C: Sure, sir. Just a moment, please.
(a few moments pass)
Here is your coat, sir. Did you enjoy our flight today?

P: Yes, it was great. Thank you.

C: You're welcome. I hope to see you on board again.

5) Other situation

Dialogue 1 Passenger moving around

C: Excuse me, sir. Would you please return to your seat and fasten your seat belt?
We will be landing shortly.

P: O.K.

C: Thank you.

Dialogue 2 Seatbelt sign on / Passenger moving around cabin

C: Excuse me, sir. As we announced, we are now making our descent to less than 10,000 feet.
Please return to your seat and fasten your seatbelt.
It's for your safety. Thank you for your understanding.

2. Disembarkation

비행기가 도착지에 안전하게 착륙하면, 안전규정상 좌석벨트 사인이 꺼질 때까지 반드시 승객이 착석하도록 하여야 한다. 좌석벨트 사인이 꺼지면 Safety check 및 Door open Sign을 주고 지상직원이 비행기 door를 Open하도록 한다.

승객의 하기 시에는, 승무원은 해당 클래스 별, 각자의 담당 구역별로 Jump seat 주변에서 승객에게 하기인사를 하고 승객 하기가 순조롭게 진행되도록 안내한다.

또한 UM, 장애인 승객, 유아 동반 승객, 노약자 승객, 짐이 많은 승객 및 운송 제한 승객 등 도움이 필요한 승객의 경우 수화물 정리를 도와드리고 비행기에서 안전하게 내릴 수 있도록 돕는다.

모든 승객 하기 후에는 잔류 승객 확인 및 승객이 놓고 내린 물건 여부를 확인한다.

1) Deplane and Farewell

Dialogue 1 승객 인사 1

C: Good bye. Thank you for flying with us.
See you again.

Dialogue 2 승객 인사 2

C: How was your flight?
P: It was wonderful. Thank you.

C: Would you make comments so that we may improve our service?

P: Everything was fine.

C: Thank you. I hope to see you again soon. Have a nice stay in Seoul.

Dialogue 3 승객 인사 3

C: Thank you for being/flying with us today. See you again.

P: Thank you. Bye.

2) Assist passenger

Dialogue 1 승객의 짐 도움

C: May I help you with your bags, ma'am?

P: No, Thank you. I can handle them.

C: (smile) Thank you for flying with us today. Good bye.

Practice 19

keeping / returning / safer / on board / fall off / fastening / flight / flying / shortly

1. Would you mind ________ your seat belt, please.
2. How was your ________?
3. We'll be landing ________.
4. It might ________ during landing.
5. Thank you for ________ with us today.
6. I hope to see you ________ again.
7. Would you mind ________ your bag under your seat until we land?
8. It will be ________ and more comfortable.

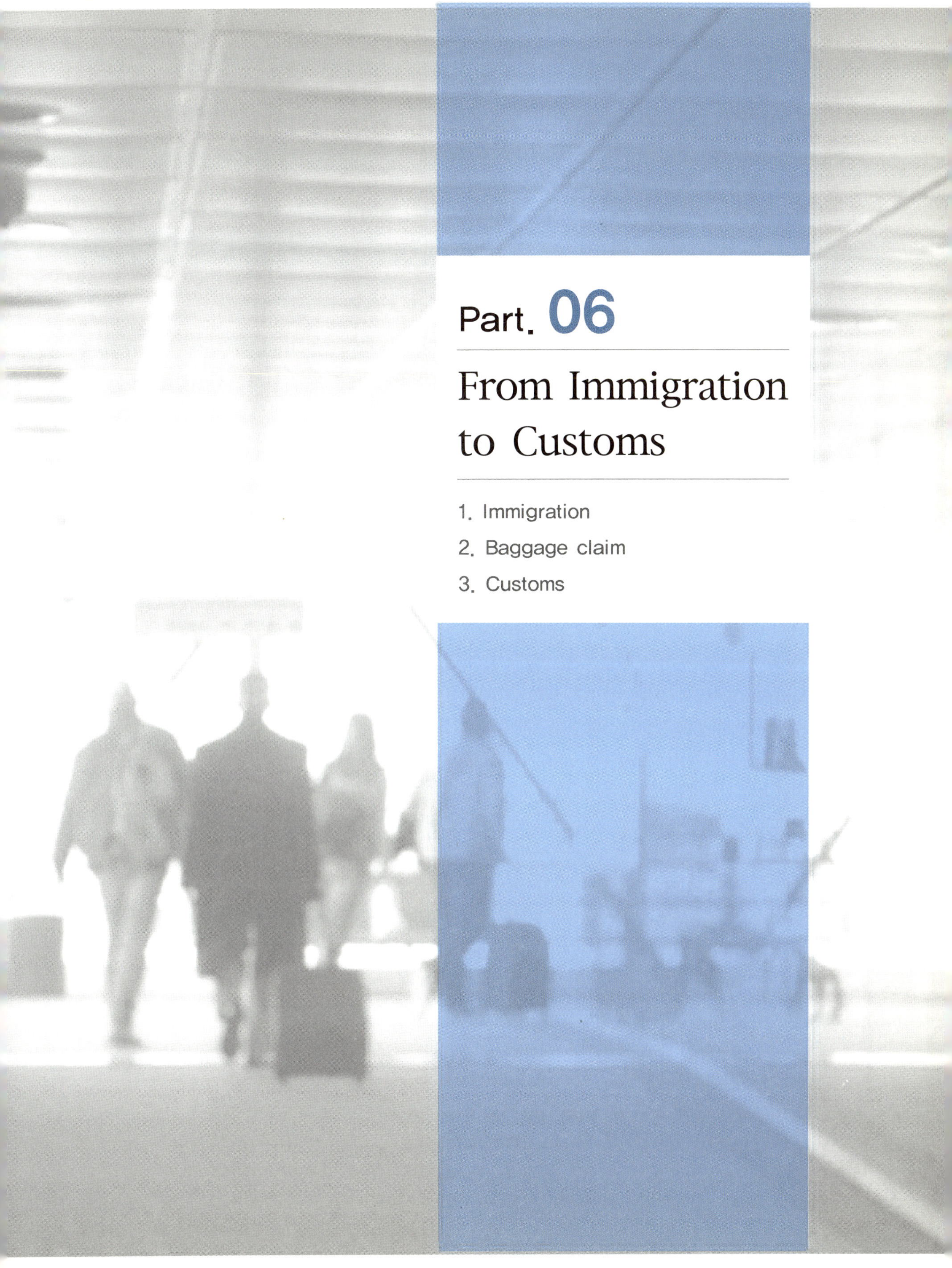

Part. 06

From Immigration to Customs

1. Immigration
2. Baggage claim
3. Customs

From Immigration to Customs

승객이 목적지 공항에 도착하여 비행기에서 내리면 해당국의 입국심사(Immigration inspection)와 세관심사(Customs inspection)를 받게 된다. 승객은 입국심사대 앞의 선 밖에서 기다리다가 차례가 되면 기내에서 받은 출입국카드(Embarkation / Disembarkation card)와 여권을 심사원에게 건네주게 된다. 입국 심사관은 입국목적(Purpose of visit), 체류기간(Length of stay), 체류지, 현금을 얼마나 갖고 있는지 등을 물어본다.

입국심사를 마친 승객은 짐 찾는 곳(Baggage claim)에서 자신의 짐을 찾아 세관검사(Customs inspection)로 향하게 된다.

간혹 짐이 도착하지 않은 경우, 항공사 직원은 승객에게 탑승권에 붙어있는 Baggage claim tag을 받아 짐의 위치를 확인 후 찾아주는 과정을 거치게 된다. 간혹 짐이 다른 비행기에 실려 엉뚱한 곳으로 가거나 출발지에서 해당 항공기에 실어지지 않았을 경우가 발생하는데, 이때에는 승객에게 정중한 사과와 함께 추후 대책을 마련해 주어야 한다.

세관 직원은 승객이 반입하는 물건 중 신고할 물건의 여부를 묻게 된다.

신고할 물건이 없으면 승객을 바로 입국시키고, 과세할 물건이 있으면 세관직원이 세액을 산출하여 지불용지를 작성해주어 승객으로 하여금 세금을 내고 물건을 찾아가게 한다.

세관 검사 시에서는 가짜 물건이나, 불법 의약품 및 동식물 검역도 같이 겸하고 있는 곳도 많다. 우선적으로는 승객이 수하물로 부친 모든 짐은 엑스레이 검사를 통해 일차로 검사가 진행되며, 추후 검사가 필요할 경우 개별적인 검사가 이뤄지기도 한다.

이후 세관을 통화하여 입국을 하게 되면, 도착 라운지(arrival hall)로 나오게 되는데, 이곳부터가 진정한 여행의 시작이라 할 수 있다.

1. Immigration

Vocabulary

- landing card
- intend
- purpose
- nationality

Key Expression

- May I see your passport and landing card, please?
- What's the purpose of your trip / visit?
- How long are you going to stay in the United States?
- Where are you going to stay?

Dialogue 1 입국심사 1

I Immigration officer / P Passenger

I: Good morning, sir. May I see your passport and landing card, please?

P: Sure. Here it is.

I: What's the purpose of your trip, sir?

P: For business.

I: How long do you intend to stay?

P: About three weeks at most.

I: (stamps the passport) O.K., sir. You may go to customs now.

P: Thank you very much.

Dialogue 2 입국심사 2

I: Passport and landing card, please.

P: Here you are.

I: What is the purpose of your visit?

P: Sightseeing.

I: How long are you going to stay in the states?

P: About two weeks.

I: Where are you going to stay in New York?

P: At the Hilton hotel.

I: Thank you. Enjoy your trip, sir.

P: Thank you.

Dialogue 3 입국심사 3

I: How long are you going to stay in the United Kingdom?

P: I'm going to stay for about 2 weeks.

I: What's the purpose of the visit?

P: I'm here on business. I work for a trading company.

I: Where are you staying?

P: I don't know my address yet. But I'm going to stay at a hotel in London.

I: How much do you have with you now?

P: I have $1,000 in traveler's check and $3,000 in cash.

I: OK. Everything seems to be in order. I hope you enjoy your stay.

P: Thank you.

Dialogue 4 입국심사 4

I: Do you live in Korea?

P: Yes, I do.

I: What's the purpose of your visit to England?

P: I'm just touring.

I: How long do you intend to stay?

P: About three weeks at most.

I: (stamps the passport) O.K., sir. You may go to customs now.

P: Thank you very much.

Frequently asked questions

1. Where did you come from? = what is your nationality = Which country are you from?
2. What's the purpose of your visit?
   A: I'm here as a tourist. / For sightseeing.
   Visiting / seeing my relatives / family / friend / daughter / son.
3. Where will you be staying in the U.S.?
   A: I'll stay at the Hilton Hotel. / I'll stay with a friend in New York.
   I'll be staying with my sister's family.

Practice 20

may / passport / long / got / trip / enjoy / purpose

1. May I see your ________ and landing card, please?
2. What's the ________ of your visit?
3. Have you _____ a visa?
4. Is this your first ______ to United states?
5. How ____________ are you going to stay in Sydney?
6. You _______ go to customs.
7. ________ your stay in New York.

2. Baggage claim

Vocabulary

- baggage claim tag
- carrousel
- claim
- come out
- contents
- conveyor (belt)
- damage (d)
- description
- file
- fill out
- lost
- pay (public) phone
- repair
- value

Key Expression

- Excuse me, where is the baggage claim area?
- I was on United Airlines Flight 005, but my bag didn't come out on the conveyor belt.
- Will you please help me to find my baggage?
- Could I see your baggage tag?
- Let me check on it. Your bag was left behind in Seoul. It will be coming in on the next flight.
- I'd like to have them repaired on your account.
- We're very sorry about your inconvenience.

Dialogue 1 짐 찾는 곳 문의 1

A Airline staff / P passenger

P: Where can I pick up luggage from Malaysia airlines flight MH064?

A: Carrousel 3.

P: Can you tell me where that is?

A: The one after this one.

Dialogue 2 | 짐 찾는 곳 문의 2

P: Excuse me, where is the baggage claim area?

A: It's downstairs on your right. You can use the escalator over there.

P: Thank you.

A: You're welcome.

Dialogue 3 | 짐 찾는 곳 문의 3

P: Excuse me. Could you please tell me where I can pick-up my bags?

O: Certainly. Which flight did you arrive on?

P: I came from Seoul, South Korea. But, I don't know the flight number.

O: No problem. Were you traveling on Korean Air?

P: That's right.

O: Then you can pick up your baggage at carousel number 11.

Dialogue 4 | 짐 분실 1

P: I was on United Airlines Flight 005, but my bag didn't come out on the conveyor belt.

A: Could I see your baggage claim tag?

P: Here it is.

A: Let me check on it.

(a few minutes pass)

Your bag was left behind in Los Angeles.

It will be coming in on the next flight, which is tomorrow morning.

Can you fill out this form?

Description of your bag, your flight number, the value of your bag's contents.

P: Oh, yes.

A: Where are you staying?

P: I'm staying at the Hotel Shilla.

A: We'll have your bag delivered there in the morning.

Dialogue 5 짐 분실 2

A: May I help you?

P: Yes, only one of my bags here.

A: How many bags did you have?

P: I had two bags.

A: Please fill out this form.

P: O.K.

A: We will inform you when we find your bag.

P: O.K. Thank you for your help.

Dialogue 6 짐 분실 3

P: Excuse me, I've been waiting for my suitcase for 40 minutes, but I can't find it.
Will you please help me to find my suitcase?

A: Sure. Can I see your baggage claim tag.

P: Yes, here you are.

A: Please wait here, I'll try to find them.

P: Thanks, but please hurry. I have only 15 minutes left to catch a plane to go to Dubai.
(a few moments pass)

A: I've located your suitcase. It was left behind in Seoul this afternoon and will arrive here tomorrow morning.

P: Oh my god! What am I supposed to do here in Singapore?

A: We are very sorry about your inconvenience.

The airline will pay expenses for you to stay in a hotel near this airport in Singapore tonight.

And you can get a flight to Dubai tomorrow morning.

P: Thanks. Where can I make a long distance call?

A: There's a pay phone over there.

Dialogue 7 짐 분실 4

P: Excuse me. I cannot find my bags.

A: Which flight were you on?

P: Singapore Airlines flight SQ700.

A: What does your baggage look like?

P: They are black suitcases with red stripes.

A: Please show me your claim tag.

P: Here you are.

A: Let me check. Unfortunately your bags have been sent to another airport, and they will arrive later today.

P: Oh, that's terrible.

A: We are very sorry about that.

Could you fill out this form with a description of your bags, the value of your bags' contents and the address where you are staying?

P: Ok. Here it is.

A: We'll deliver your bags there tonight.

Dialogue 8 짐 분실 5

P: Hello, I've just arrived from London, but my baggage is missing.

A: I see. May I see your baggage claim tags, please?

P: Yes, here they are.

A: Would you fill out this form while we trace your baggage?

P: Sure. When can I get my baggage?

A: Your baggage will arrive on the next flight from London.

P: Should I collect my baggage here?

A: No. We will deliver it to the address you give.

Dialogue 9 Describing missing baggage

A: How many bags are you missing?

P: One.

A: Could you please describe it for me?

P: Oh, it's a regular suitcase with wheels.

A: What color is it?

P: It's dark green.

A: What size is it?

P: It's medium sized. Where can I pick up my bag?

A: It'll be delivered to your address.

Dialogue 10 Damaged baggage(짐 훼손)

A: What can I do for you, sir?

P: My baggage is somewhat damaged.
I'd like to have them repaired on your account.

A: We're very sorry about your inconvenience.
I will file a claim for you.

P: Thank you very much. But I'd like to have them repaired as soon as possible.

Dialogue 11 가방 바뀜

A: May I help you?

P: I hope so.

A: What can I do for you?

P: I picked up the wrong bag by mistake. It looked just like mine.

A: What is the name on the bag?

P: Mr. John Simpson.

A: I'll page Mr. Simpson and have him report here.

P: That would be great. Perhaps he has my bag.

Practice 21

repaired / sorry / claim / check / left / tag / help / conveyor

1. Excuse me, where is the baggage ______ area?
2. I was on United Airlines Flight 005, but my bag didn't come out on the __________ belt.
3. Will you please _________ me to find my baggage?
4. Could I see your baggage ____?
5. Let me ________ on it. Your bag was ________ behind in Seoul. It will be coming in on the next flight.
6. I'd like to have them ________ on your account.
7. We're very ________ about your inconvenience.

3. Customs

Key Expression

- May I see your customs declaration form, please?
- Do you have anything to declare?
- What do you have in your suitcase?
- Would you open your bag, please?

Dialogue 1 Customs(세관통과 1)

C Customs officer / P Passenger

C: May I see your customs declaration form, please?

P: Yes, here you are.

C: Do you have anything to declare?

P: No, nothing.

C: What do you have in your suitcase?

P: Just some clothes and books.

C: Would you open your suitcase, please?

P: Certainly.

C: O.K. everything is cleared. You may go now.

P: Thank you.

Dialogue 2 Customs(세관통과 2)

C: Do you have anything to declare?

P: No, I have nothing to declare.

C: Do you have any alcoholic beverages or tobacco?

P: I have some cigarettes, but just for my own use.

C: What is this?

P: They are gifts for my family.

C: You may proceed.

P: Thank you.

Dialogue 3 Customs(세관통과 3)

C: Do you have anything to declare, sir?

P: What kind of items do I have to declare?

C: Well, fruits, plants, animals, jewelry and so on.
What do you have in this suitcase?

P: Books, cloths, shoes and some personal effects.

C: Do you have anything more besides that?

P: No.

C: All right. That's all. You may go now, sir.

P: Thank you.

Dialogue 4 Customs(세관통과 4)

C: Do you have anything to declare?

P: No I don't.

C: Please hand me the customs declaration form.

P: Here it is.

C: Open your baggage, please.

P: OK. I only have personal items.

C: You may go out by following the green line.

P: Thank you.

Dialogue 5 Customs(세관통과 5)

C: Do you have anything to declare?

P: No, nothing.

C: Do you have any fruits, plants, vegetables, or meat?

P: No, I don't. But I have some wine.

C: How much wine do you have?

P: I only have a bottle.

C: That's okay. Please proceed to the exit marked "Nothing to declare".

P: Thank you.

Practice 22

open / have / declare / customs declaration

1. Do you have anything to ________?
2. May I see your ________________________, please?
3. What do you ________ in your suitcase?
4. Will you ________ your bag, please?

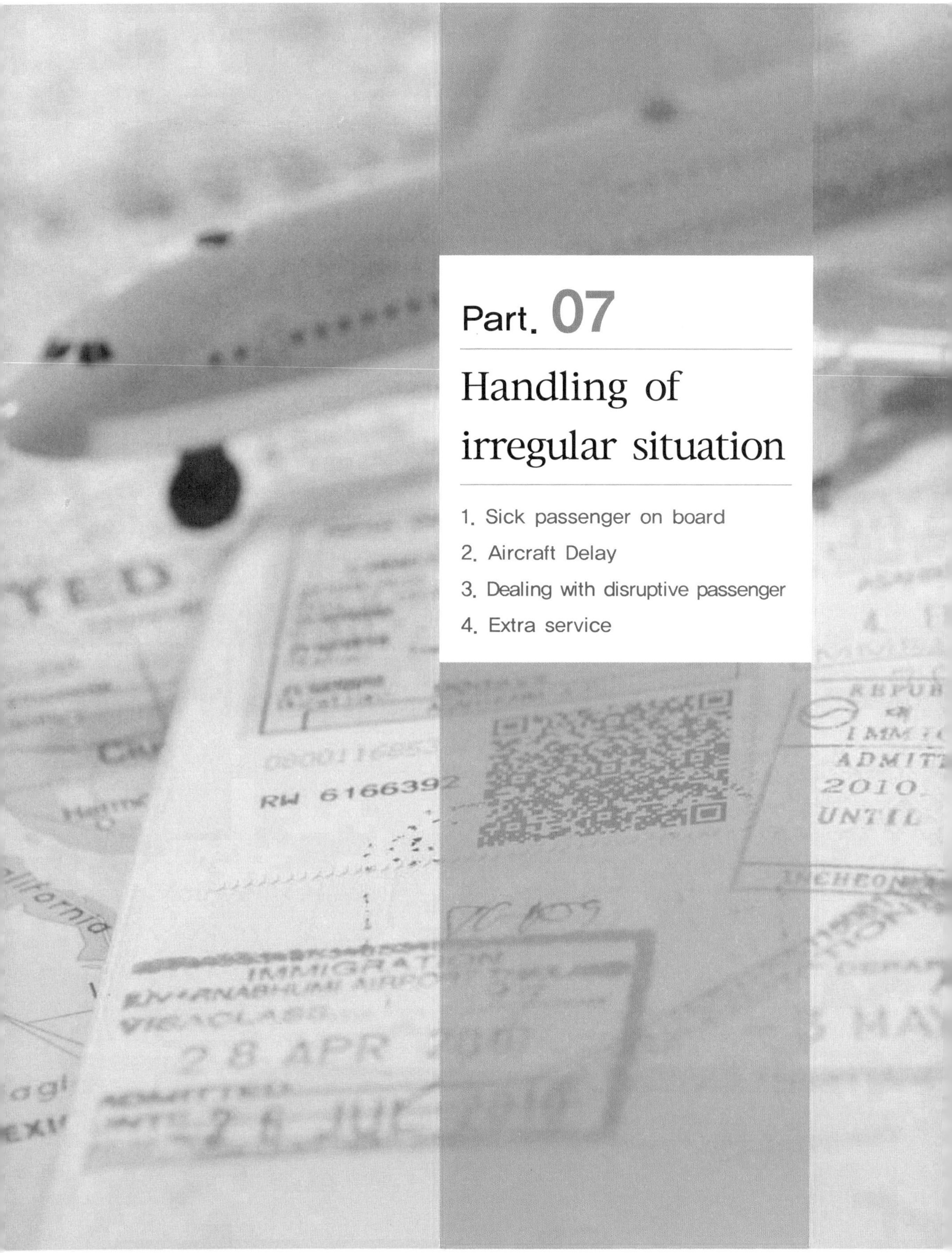

Part. 07

Handling of irregular situation

1. Sick passenger on board
2. Aircraft Delay
3. Dealing with disruptive passenger
4. Extra service

Part 7

Handling of irregular situation

본 장에서는 기내에서 발생할 수 있는 기타 상황에 대해 정리하였다. 일반적인 상황이 아닌 갑작스런 상황이 발생했을 때, 가장 중요한 것은 신속한 응대와 팀 내 커뮤니케이션을 긴밀하게 유지하는 것이라 할 수 있다.

1. Sick passenger on board

손님의 입장에서 항공기 여행 중에 가장 괴로운 순간의 하나는 갑작스런 몸의 이상증상일 것이다.

비행기 안에서 자주 발생하는 손님들의 건강상 문제는 소화불량, 설사, 감기, 발열 등이 있는데, 비행기를 타고 이동하는 상태에서 발생한 갑작스러운 건강상의 문제는 손님의 여행일정 및 정서에 적지 않은 문제를 초래할 수 있다. 그러므로 아픈 승객들을 위한 세심한 서비스가 필요하다.

비행 중 갑작스럽게 발생한 환자의 응급조치를 위해 기내에는 멀미약, 감기약, 소화제 등 비상 약들이 구비되어 있고, 승무원들은 손님들이 아플 때 어떻게 조치를 취해야 하는지 잘 숙지하고 있다 할 수 있다.

빈번하진 않지만, 심각한 환자 발생 시에는 근처공항 또는 출발지로 회항하기도 한다. 이 모든 상황에 신속한 대처를 위해 승무원들은 절차상의 조치 문제나, 환자 발생 시 대처방법 등을 잘 숙지하고 있어야 하며, 또한 팀원 간의 커뮤니케이션을 원활하게 유지할 수 있도록 해야 한다.

Vocabulary

- airsick
- diarrhea
- heartburn
- nauseous
- sore / sore throat
- upset stomach
- anti-
- dry
- indigestion
- provide
- swallowing
- yawing
- block
- first aid
- medicine
- sick
- throwing up

Key Expression

- Do you have anything I can take?
- Do you have any medicine?
- Try swallowing hard.
- Try yawning.
- Hold your nose and mouth and blow out gently.

Dialogue 1 멀미손님(출발 전)

P: Excuse me. I get airsick really easily. Do you have anything for that?

C: Yes, we have some anti-airsickness medicine. Would that be alright, sir?

P: Yes, thanks.

F: Here you are. I hope you feel better.

Sick passenger

Excuse me. I feel nauseous.
I have indigestion / an upset stomach.
I have heartburn.
I have diarrhea.
Do you have anything I can take?
Do you have any medicine?
Can I have some medicine, please?

Dialogue 2 멀미손님(비행 중)

P: Excuse me, I feel like vomiting / I feel like throwing up.

C: Here is an airsick bag for you just in case you vomit, ma'am.
Is there anything that I can do for you?

P: Do you have anything I can take?

C: Yes, we have air sickness pills on board. Would that be alright?

P: Yes, please.

C: Just a moment, please.
(a few moments pass)
Here's your medicine.

P: Thanks a lot.

C: My pleasure. I hope you feel better.
(later)

C: How are you feeling, ma'am?

P: I feel better. Thanks.

C: You're welcome. I'm glad to hear that. Can I get you anything else?

P: No, thanks.

Dialogue 3 Sore throat

P: Excuse me. The air in here is so dry and my throat has become a little sore.
Do you have any medicine?

C: I'm sorry, sir. We don't have anything for a sore throat.
Would you care for some hot tea with lemon?

P: Yes, please.

C: Just a moment, please. Here is your tea. I hope you feel better.

Dialogue 4 Headache

P: Excuse me. Do you have any medicine for a headache?

C: Yes, we do. We have Panadol for headaches.
Are you allegic to Asprin?

P: No. Can I have Panadol then?

C: Certainly, ma'am.
(a few moments pass)
Ma'am, Here is your medicine.

P: Thank you.

C: You're welcome. I hope you feel better. Jest relax.

Dialogue 5 Diarrhea

P: Excuse me. Do you have anything for diarrhea?

C: Yes, we do. We have Jungkrohwhan, a Korean medicine, for diarrhea.
Have you tried it before?

P: No, I haven't. But I'll try that.

C: O.K. sir. Please give me a minute.
(a few minutes pass)
Here you are. If I can get you anything else, please let me know.

Dialogue 6 Blocked ears

P: Excuse me. A sudden pressure change in the cabin has blocked my ears.
What do I do?

C: Do you have a cold?

P: Yes, I do.

C: Why don't you try swallowing hard. Are you all right now?
Then try yawning.

Or

P: No, I don't.

C: Then try holding your nose and with your mouth closed blow out gently.

P: Thanks. That worked.

C: You're welcome.

Practice 23

blocked / vomit / feeling / get / tried

1. I ______ airsick really easily.
2. Here is an airsick bag for you just in case you ________, ma'am.
3. How are you __________ , ma'am?
4. Have you ________ it before?
5. The change in cabin pressure _________ my ears.

2. Aircraft Delay

비행기가 지연되는 이유에는 항공사 문제, 공항의 문제, 승객의 탑승 문제 등의 여러 가지 원인이 있는데, 이러한 지연에 대해 안내를 할 때에는 승객에게 불편을 드리는 것이므로 사과의 말로 양해를 구하는 것이 우선이며, 그 후에 지연 이유에 대한 설명을 해야 한다.

Vocabulary

- delay
- hold-up
- loaded

Key Expression

- We're waiting for a few more passengers to come on board.
- It will take us about 15 minutes to take-off.
- We're waiting for the baggage to be loaded.
- We'll be taking off as soon as they arrive.

Dialogue 1 Delay in Departure 1

P: Why is there a delay?

C: I'm sorry, ma'am. We're waiting for a few more passengers to come on board.
We'll be taking off as soon as they arrive.

Dialogue 2 Delay in Departure 2

P: What's the reason for the delay?

C: I'm sorry, ma'am. We're waiting for the baggage to be loaded.

Dialogue 3 Delay in Departure 3

C: I'm sorry sir. Our take-off has been delayed because we have so many airplanes in front of us that are waiting to take-off.
We are 7th in line and it will take us about 10 minutes to take-off.
We are sorry for the inconvenience.

Dialogue 4 Delay in Departure 4

P: What's the hold-up?

C: I'm sorry, sir. Our take-off has been delayed because we have so many airplanes in front of us that are waiting to take-off.
It will take us about 15 minutes to take-off.

Practice 24

loaded / few more / as soon as / take

1. We're waiting for a _____ ______ passengers to come on board.
2. It will _____ us about 15 minutes to take-off.
3. We're waiting for the baggage to be_________.
4. We'll be taking off ________________ they arrive.

3. Dealing with disruptive passenger

안전한 항공기 운항에 지장을 주는 승객이 있을 경우, 이때에는 무엇보다도 승무원의 단호한 태도가 중요하다. 이는 서비스보다 승객과 항공기의 안전이 무엇보다 중요하기 때문이다. 특히 외국항공사는 안전에 영향을 미칠 수 있는 행동을 하는 승객에게 무척 단호한 태도를 취한다고 할 수 있다.

Vocabulary

- against
- cooperation
- put out
- turn off
- aviation law
- effect
- step out
- compliance
- prohibited
- strictly

Key Expression

- Please put out the cigarette and step out of the lavatory.
- Smoking on board is against aviation law.
- Using a mobile-phone is strictly prohibited during the whole flight.
- Would you please turn it off now?
- Thank you for your cooperation.
- Because of cabin pressure, the effects of alcohol are stronger in the air.

Dialogue 1 Passenger smoking in lavatory

C: Excuse me, sir. Did you smoke? Please put out the cigarette and step out of the lavatory.

Smoking on board is against aviation law, we need to report you to the captain and the airport police.

Dialogue 2 Passenger using cell-phone

C: Excuse me, sir. Using a cell (mobile)-phone is strictly prohibited during the whole flight.

Would you please turn it off now?

It's for the safe operation of our flight and it's in compliance with aviation law.

Thank you for your cooperation.

Dialogue 3 Drunken passenger wants another drink

P: Give me another whisky.

C: I'm sorry, sir.

We can't serve you any more alcoholic beverages.

You've already had 4 glasses of Vodka.

Please remember, because of cabin pressure, the effects of alcohol are stronger in the air.

Would you care for a non-alcoholic beverage instead?

Practice 25

against / step out / strictly / turn / cooperation / off / effects / step out / put out

1. Please __________ the cigarette and ___________ of the lavatory.
2. Smoking on board is ___________ aviation law.
3. Using a mobile-phone is ______ prohibited during the whole flight.
4. Would you please _______ it _____off now?
5. Thank you for your. ____________.
6. Because of cabin pressure, the __________ of alcohol are stronger in the air.

4. Extra service

Vocabulary

• a deck of cards	• adjust	• armrest
• bear with	• blanket	• knob
• lean back	• lean forward	• lie down
• light bulb	• pass through	• stretch out
• uncomfortable	• ventilation	

Key Expression

- Would you like a blanket, sir?
- Would you like to lie down?
- Would you like to pass through first?
- Do you have a deck of cards?
- To open it please turn the knob to the right, sir.
- Please press the button that looks like a light bulb.
- To recline, just push this button and lean back. And to the upright position, push the button and lean forward.

1) Passenger comfort

Dialogue 1 Cabin service

C: Would you like a blanket, sir?

P: Yes. Please.

C: And here's a pillow. Would you care for some hot tea or coffee, sir?

P: No, thanks.

C: Alright, sir. Have a good rest.

Dialogue 2 Stretch out / Row available

C: Excuse, ma'am. Would you like to lie down?
We have an empty row in the middle of the cabin. Would that be alright, ma'am?

P: Oh, yes. Thank you.

C: This way, ma'am. Here is your seat.
Would you like a pillow and a blanket?

P: Yes, thank you.

F: You're welcome. Have a good rest, ma'am.

2) Other situation

Dialogue 1 When faced with a passenger in the aisle

C: Ma'am. Would you like to pass through first?
Or
Would you like to pass through?
Let me remove the cart, just a minutes please.
Thank you. (If cabin attendant goes through first)

Dialogue 2 Baby continues to cry in the cabin

C: May I help you? If you need anything, please feel free to let us know.
Or
F: Excuse me. May I hold your baby?
It's hard for adults to travel long distances and this baby is behaving very well.
If you need assistance at any time, please let us know.
We will be glad to help.

Dialogue 3 시끄럽게 떠드는 어린이 손님

P1: Excuse me. I'm trying to get some rest, but that little boy is making so much noise.
Can you do something about it.
C: I'm sorry for the inconvenience. Just a moment, please.
(to little boy)
C: Hi! What's your name?
P2: Tim.
C: How old are you?

P2: Four.

C: Do you want some orange juice?

P2: Yes.

C: I see. You're being very good! Where is your seat, Tim?

Dialogue 4 Passenger comfort

C: (with a smile) Are you enjoying the flight, sir?

P: I guess so.

C: Would you care for some coffee?

P: Yes, please. How long will it be before we get to Washington, D.C.?

C: We expect to arrive in about three hours.

P: I see.

C: Would you care for a newspaper or magazine?

P: Do you have "The Times?"

C: Certainly, sir. Just a moment, please.

(a few moments pass)

Here is the magazine you requested, sir.

P: Thank you very much.

C: My pleasure.

Dialogue 5 신혼부부 사진촬영 요구

P: Excuse me. Would you mind taking our picture? We're on our honeymoon.

C: Oh, really? Congratulations! I'd be glad to take your picture.

P: Just push this button, please.

C: All right. Are you ready? Cheese! There you go.

P: Thank you very much.

C: You're welcome.

I hope you have a wonderful honeymoon.

Dialogue 6 Passenger asks for a deck of cards

C: Do you need something, sir?

P: Yes, do you have a deck of cards?

C: Yes. We do have some.

P: Could we have two decks, please?

C: I'll bring them right away.

P: Great!

C: Here they are, sir. Have fun.

P: Thanks, this will help the time go quickly.

3) Aircraft Service unit

Dialogue 1 사용법을 모르는 손님 1

P: Excuse me. How do I adjust the ventilation?

C: To open it please turn the knob to the right, sir.

P: And how do I adjust the volume?

C: (Armrest에 부착되어 있는 button을 가리키며)
You may just press this button.
Do you know how to change channels?

P: I have no idea.

C: (Armrest에 부착되어 있는 button을 가리키며) Just press this button, sir.

P: Will you show me how to use the reading light?

C: (좌석 위에 부착된 Panel이나 / Armrest에 있는 button을 가리키며)
Please press the button that looks like a light bulb.

P: Thank you.

C: You're welcome.

Dialogue 2 사용법을 모르는 손님 2

P: Where can I plug in the earphone set?

C: (Armrest에 earphone jack을 가리키며) Right here, sir.

P: Thank you. And I have another question.
How do I recline my seat and return it to the upright position?

C: (Armrest에 위치한 button을 가리키며)
To recline, just push this button and lean back. And to the upright position, push the button and lean forward.

P: Thank you very much.

C: You're welcome.

Dialogue 3 Resetting entertainment system

P: Excuse me. Something is wrong. I can't hear and watch anything now.
What am I supposed to do?

C: Sir, We are having a problem with our in-flight entertainment system.
So, we are restarting the system now. Would you please bear with us?
It will be ready in a minute. I'm sorry for the inconvenience.

P: Oh, I see.

Practice 26

through / lie down / knob / lean back / deck / like / pass / press / recline

1. Would you ______ a blanket, sir?
2. Would you like to ____________?
3. Would you like to _____ __________first?
4. Do you have a ______ of cards?
5. To open it please turn the ______ to the right, sir.
6. Please _______ the button that looks like a light bulb.
7. To______, just push this button and ___________.

부 록

In-flight announcement

1. 국내 항공사 A
2. 국내항공사 B
3. 국내항공사 C
4. 유럽 항공사 A
5. 유럽 항공사 B
6. 중동 항공사
7. 동남아 항공사 A
8. 동남아 항공사 B

부 록

In-flight announcement

기내방송은 비행 전반에 대한 내용을 승객에게 전달하는 매우 중요한 승무원의 업무 중 하나이다. 기내방송은 서비스 절차, 안전사항, 항로정보 등의 내용을 승객에게 적절한 시기에 정확하게 전달하는 것이 중요한데, 이때 듣는 사람의 입장에서 잘 들릴 수 있도록 볼륨 및 발음을 잘 조절하는 것도 매우 중요하다.

기내방송 시 유의사항

1. 항공기별로 마이크 감도 및 음량이 다르므로 비행 전에 PA(Public Announcement) system의 상태를 반드시 점검한다.
2. 방송 시 PA 기기의 음량은 대체로 대화하는 수준이거나 또는 그보다 다소 낮은 목소리로 명료하게 방송한다. 일부러 큰 소리를 낼 필요는 없다.
3. 발음은 정확하게, 또한 쉴 곳과 강조해야 할 부분을 구분하여 방송한다.
4. PA 기기를 통해 숨소리나 바람소리 등의 잡음이 나가지 않도록 해야 한다.
5. 갑자기 큰소리로 방송하여 손님을 놀라게 하지 않아야 한다.
6. 항공사에서 기본으로 제공하는 기본 방송문을 토대로 하여 최대한의 신선미를 가미한 자율적인 방송을 하되, 너무 길지 않고 정중한 문구를 구사하도록 한다.
7. 콧소리를 내거나 발음과 억양에 있어 반복적이거나 끝을 늘리거나 과도하게 올리는 등의 거부감을 줄 수 있는 방송은 피한다.
8. '비상사태', '악천후', '엔진이상', '번개', '계기이상' 등의 안전과 관련되어 승객들에게 집단 불안감을 심어줄 수 있는 용어는 절대 사용해서는 안 된다.

1. 국내 항공사 A

1) Baggage securing

Ladies and gentlemen,

Thank you for flying with us today. This is __________ flight _________ bound for _________.

For your safety, please place your carry-on items in the overhead bins or under the seat in front of you. Thank you.

2) Preparation for departure

Ladies and gentlemen,

This is __________ flight ______ bound for ______.

We are now just (a few/____) minutes away from an on-time departure.

Please make sure that your carry-on items are stored in the overhead bins or under the seat in front of you.

Also, please take your assigned seat and fasten your seat belt. Thank you.

3) Welcome

Good morning (afternoon/evening), ladies and gentlemen(and boys an girls)

Captain (Family name) and the entire crew/ would like to welcome you onboard _______________.

This is flight ____bound for____(via____).

Our flight time today will be ____hour(s) and ____minute(s) after take off.

During the flight, our cabin crew will be happy to serve you in any way we can.

We wish you an enjoyable flight.

And please direct your attention for a few minutes to the (video screens / cabin crew) for safety information.

4) Seat belt sign off

Ladies and gentlemen, The Captain has turned off the seat belt sign.
In case of any unexpected turbulence, we strongly recommend you keep your seat belt fastened at all times while seated.
Please use caution when opening the overhead bins as the contents may fall out.
Thank you.

5) Service procedure

Ladies and gentlemen,
We would like to briefly inform you about our service today.
We will begin our in flight service staring with beverages, and (breakfast/ lunch/dinner/a light meal) will follow.
Also, in-flight sales will begin after the meal service is completed.
And, approximately ____hour(s) ____minute(s) prior to landing, (breakfast/ lunch/dinner/a light meal)will be served.
We hope you understand that your meal choice may not be available.
Thank you for choosing ____________, have a pleasant flight.

6) Turbulence

Ladies and gentlemen, We are continuing to experience the turbulence.
For your safety, please remain seated with your seatbelt fastened.
Thank you.

7) In-flight sales

Ladies and gentlemen,
Our in-flight duty free sales have started and you may now purchase duty-free items, or order items of your return flight.

For more information, please refer to the in-flight sales magazine in your seat pocket.

(DUTY FREE ALLOWANCE)

We would like to remind you that the duty free allowance for (country) is ____bottle(s) Of liquor and ____carton(s) of cigarettes.

If you need any assistance, our cabin crew is happy to help you.

8) Movie

Ladies and gentlemen, Our film(s) today is (are) ____(and____).

As a courtesy to other passengers, we ask you to please close your window shades, and in case of any unexpected turbulence, please remember to keep your seat belt fastened while seated.

9) Transit procedure

Ladies and gentlemen,

Passengers continuing to ____with us should collect a transit card after leaving the airplane, and then proceed to the transit area.

For security reason you must take all your belongings with you.

Our scheduled departure time for ____is ____ (am/pm).

We will started re-boarding in about ____minutes.

Please listen for a boarding announcement in the transit area. Thank you.

10) Headphone collection

Ladies and gentlemen,

Our cabin crew will be coming through the cabin to collect your headphones.

Also, we ask you to please leave your blanket in your seat pocket.

Thank you for your cooperation.

11) Approaching

Ladies and gentlemen, We are approaching ____airport.
At this time, we ask you to please store your carry-on items in the overhead bins or under the seat in front of you.
Thank you for your cooperation.

12) Landing

Ladies and gentlemen, We will be landing shortly.
In preparation for landing, please fasten your seat belt, return your seat and tray table to the upright position, and open your window shades.
Also, please discontinue the use of electronic devices until the aircraft has been parked at the gate.
Thank you.

13) Farewell

Ladies and gentlemen, We have landed at(공항명) (international) airport.
The local time is now (__:__) am/pm, (month) (date), and the temperature is ____degrees Celsius or ____degrees Fahrenheit.
Thank you for choosing ____________ and we hope to see you again soon on your next flight.

2. 국내항공사 B

1) Baggage Securing

Ladies and Gentlemen, This is ________ Airlines flight ________ bound for ______.
For your comfort and safety, please put your carry-on baggage in the

overhead bins or under the seat in front of you.
When you open the overhead bins, please be careful as the contents may fall out.
Thank you.

2) Welcome announcement

Good morning (afternoon / evening), Ladies and Gentlemen.
Captain ________ and the entire crew would like to welcome you aboard _______ Airlines flight ________(flight no.) bound for _______(destination).
Our flight time will be ____ hour(s) ____ minutes following take off.
Please make sure your seat belt is securely fastened.
And please return your seat and tray table to their upright position.
The use of electronic devices including a mobile phone is not allowed during take-off and landing.
Smoking in the cabin and lavatories is prohibited at all times during the flight.
We are pleased to have you on board today and we'll do our very best to serve you.
Thank you.

3) Safety Video showing

Ladies and Gentlemen.
We'd like to familiarize you with the safety features of this aircraft.
Please take moment to view the following video program.
Thank you.

4) Seat belt sign off

Ladies and Gentlemen.

Although the seat belt sign has been turned off, in case of sudden turbulence, please keep your seat belt fastened at all times during the flight.
When opening the overhead bins, be careful as the contents may fall out.
You may now use CD Players and laptop computers.
For further information on the type of electronic devices allowed on board please refer to magazine in your seat pocket.
We'd like to remind you that smoking is prohibited in the cabin and lavatories.
Your cooperation is much appreciated.
Thank you.

5) Turbulence (general)

Ladies and Gentlemen,
* We are expecting some turbulence.
* We are experiencing some turbulence.

Please fasten (keep) your seatbelt (fastened) until the captain turns off the seatbelt sign.
Thank you.

6) Turbulence(서비스 중지)

Ladies and Gentlemen, as we are experiencing turbulence, hot beverage (meal) services will be delayed until the condition is improved.
* We'll continue all services as soon as the turbulence subsides.
* We'll continue hot beverage service as soon as possible.
* Due to the turbulence, we can not complete hot beverage (meal) service before landing.

We are sorry for this inconvenience.

7) Landing

Ladies and Gentlemen,
We will be landing shortly.
Please stow your carry-on baggage and return your seat back, and tray table to the upright position.
Also please check that your seat belt is fastened and discontinue the use of all electronic devices until the aircraft is parked at the gate.
Thank you for your cooperation.

8) Farewell

Ladies and Gentlemen,
We have just landed at ______ airport.
The local time is ______ AM/PM.
For your safety, we request that you remain seated until the captain turns off the seat belt sign.
Also, refrain from using your mobile phone until you deplane.
When opening the overhead bins, please be careful as the contents may fall out.
Before leaving the aircraft, please check that there's no items left in your seat pocket or under your seat. Please take all carry-on baggage with you when you deplane.
On behalf of entire crew, we've enjoyed serving you today and we hope to see you soon.
Thank you.

3. 국내항공사 C

1) Baggage

Ladies and gentlemen,

This is _______ flight _______ bound for _______.

For your safety and comfort, please put your carry-on baggage in the overhead bins or under the seat in front of you.

When you open the overhead bins, please be careful as the baggage may fall out.

Also, please turn off all electronic devices including mobile phones with flight mode.

Thank you for your cooperation.

2) Welcome

Good morning (afternoon/evening) ladies and gentlemen,

on behalf of Captain _________ and the entire crew, we would like to welcome you on board _________ flight _________ bound for _________.

Our flight time to(공항명)(int'l) airport will be 00 hour 00 minutes after take-off.

For departure, please fasten your seat belt, put your seat upright and secure your tray table.

Also, all electronic devices including mobile phones with flight mode should be turned off during take-off and landing.

We wish you a pleasant flight.

Thank you.

3) Take-off

Ladies and gentlemen, we are about to take - off.
Please make sure that your seat belt is securely fastened.
Thank you for your cooperation.

4) Seat belt sign off

Ladies and gentlemen, The seatbelt sign is now off.
However, for your safety, please keep your seatbelt fastened while seated.
And we'd like to inform that you can use the electronic devices from now.
Thank you for your cooperation.

5) C.I.Q forms

Ladies and gentlemen, we will be distributing the entry documents for(국가명).
All passengers entering(국가명) are kindly requested to fill out the forms completely.

6) Turbulence

Ladies and gentlemen,
a. [Turbulence 조우 시] we are now passing through turbulence.
b. [Turbulence 예상 시] we will be passing through turbulence.
Please return to your seat and fasten your seat belt.
Also, please refrain from using the lavatories until the seat belt sign is off.
Thank you for your cooperation.

7) In-flight sales

Ladies and gentlemen,

(항공사 이름) has prepared a variety of duty free items for your convenience. We have many duty free items and if you are interested, please inform one of our cabin crew.
Also you can pre-order a product and pick it up on your return flight.
For further information, please review the Eastar jet SKY SHOP shopping guide in your seat pocket.
Thank you.

8) Dimming lights

Ladies and gentlemen,
for your comfort, we will be dimming the cabin lights.
If you would like to read, the reading light is above your head.

9) Cabin cleaning & Approaching

Ladies and gentlemen,
we are approaching ________ (int'l) airport.
Please stow your carry-on baggage, fasten your seat belt, return your seat back, tray table and open your window shade.
Also all electronic devices including mobile phones with flight mode should be turned off at this time.
[필요한 경우]
For your pleasant flight, please pass used cups and waste items to our cabin crew.
Thank you.

10) Landing

Ladies and gentlemen, we will be landing shortly.
Please make sure that your seat belt is securely fastened.
Thank you for your cooperation.

11) Good-bye (Farewell)

Ladies and gentlemen,

Welcome to ______________ international airport.

The local time here is (___:___) AM/PM

For your safety, please remain seated until the aircraft has come to a complete stop and the captain has turned off the seatbelt sign.

And you can use the electronic devices only outside of the aircraft.

On behalf of(항공사 이름), we would like to thank you for allowing us to serve you and we hope to see you again soon.

12) Deplane

Thank you for waiting, ladies and gentlemen.

You may now exit the aircraft by using the front door on the left.

Please check again your personal belongings before you deplane.

Thank you and good bye.

4. 유럽 항공사 A

1) Welcome on board

Ladies and Gentlemen,

My name is __________ (and together with ___________), I am/we are your purser(s) on today's flight.

All of us in the cabin crew hope to make your stay with us a pleasant and relaxing one.

It is my pleasure to add my welcome to that of the captain on this _____ airlines flight __________ service to __________(via__________).

We will fly you to __________ today in _____ hours.

The doors are now closed and we will soon be on our way.
Please make certain that cell phones and all other electronic equipment are switched off.
May we ask you to direct your attention to the cabin screens for a film that will acquaint you with the safety features of this aircraft.
If you have any questions, please contact one of the cabin attendants.
Thank you for your attention, and we are looking forward to this flight with you.

2) Service Information

Ladies and Gentlemen,
Once we have reached our cruising altitude, we shall be serving drinks, followed by a hot lunch/dinner/breakfast.
Afterwards you will be able to buy a selection of items at reduced prices from our in-flight shopping service,
Before landing, we will be serving dinner/breakfast/a light snack.
If you have any questions or requests, we will be happy to help you.
On your flight today, we have flight attendants who speak English, _____ and __________.
Ladies and Gentlemen, we now invite you to sit back, relax and enjoy your flight with us.

3) Documentation

Ladies and Gentlemen,
We will now be distributing the immigration forms for __________.
After you have filled them in, please keep them with your passport.

4) Turbulences

Ladies and Gentlemen,
As you will have noticed, we are passing through an area of turbulence. Please make sure that your seat belts are fastened. Thank you

5) Medical assistance

Ladies and Gentlemen,
May we have your attention.
One of our passengers urgently requires medical assistance.
Would all doctors on board please contact us immediately. Thank you

6) Approach

Ladies and Gentlemen, We are starting our approach.
Please make sure that your seat belts are fastened and that your hand baggage is stowed safely.
It is essential that you switch off your electronic equipment before landing.
It may only be used again when the "fasten seat belt" signs are turned off.
Thank you

7) Shortly before landing

Ladies and Gentlemen,
Please ensure that your seat is in the upright position and your table is folded away.
If your seat has a foot rest and retractable monitor, stow them away.
Thank you.

8) Farewell

We welcome you to ____________, Ladies and Gentlemen, where the local time is ______________.

Please remember to keep your seat belt fastened until the seat belt sign above your head has been switched off.

Captain ______ and the entire crew would like to take this opportunity to thank you for travelling with us and wish you a pleasant stay here in ______ and a safe onward journey.

Thank you and good bye.

5. 유럽 항공사 B

1) Welcome announcement

Good morning (afternoon / evening) Ladies and Gentlemen.

The name of our (senior) purser on this flight there are cabin crew members who speak the Korean language.

On behalf of Captain _________ and the crew I'd like to welcome you on board.

This is the flight to ________. We expect to depart shortly.

Our flying time will be ____ hours and ____ minutes.

Ladies and Gentlemen, please switch off your cell phones and stow them.

In a few minutes, we will show you a video about the safety provisions on board.

2) Fasten seatbelt sign switched off

Ladies and Gentlemen,

The 'fasten seatbelt' sign has been switched off. However, we advise you to keep your seatbelt fastened while seated.

3) Before Landing

Ladies and Gentlemen, we are approaching ______ airport in ________.
Local time is _______ AM/PM.
Kindly stow your carry-on luggage in the overhead bins or under the seat in front of you. If you are using electronic equipment, please switch it off and stow it,
Please fasten your seatbelts, adjust the back of your seats to the upright position and fold away your tray tables. Also fold away any footrests and video screens in use.
For your own safety, make sure no blankets are blocking access to the aisles.
Thank you.

4) Farewell

Welcome to _______.
Please remain seated until the fasten seatbelt signs have been switched off.
Remember to remove any personal belongings from your seat pocket and the overhead bins before leaving the aircraft.
Please be careful when opening the overhead bins. Luggage may fall out unexpectedly.
We'd like to say goodbye now. On behalf of ______ and ______, thank you for flying with us and we hope to see you again on board.
If ______ is your final destination, we'd like to wish you a pleasant stay.
If you're traveling further, we wish you a pleasant continuation of your journey.

6. 중동 항공사

1) Welcome announcement

Good Morning / Afternoon / Evening Ladies and Gentlemen, my name is ______________ and I am your Purser today. On behalf of the Cabin Crew Team I would like to welcome you onboard this __________ airlines flight to __________.

We are now departing to _________, may I ask you to please turn off your mobile phone and ensure it remains switched off until otherwise advised by the crew. Thank you.

2) Safety Demo with Video

In a few moments, I will be showing a short video on the safety aspects of this aircraft. Please watch and listen carefully.

3) Turbulence

As we are passing through an area of rough air, please return to your seat and make sure that your seat belt is tightly fastened.

4) Pre Landing

As we shall shortly be arriving at __________ would you please return to your seat. Make sure your hand baggage is placed under the seat in front of you or in the overhead locker and that your seat back is upright with the armrest down. Window blinds should be open, tray tables and footrests should be folded and stowed and your seatbelt securely fastened. To ensure you are fully aware of the exit nearest to you and the safety features on this aircraft, read the Safety Procedures Card in your seat pocket. If you have been using your Personal Electronic Devices, please ensure that they are now switched off.

5) After Landing

Ladies and Gentlemen,

Welcome to ______________ where the local time is __________ and the temperature is _____ degrees centigrade or _____ degrees Fahrenheit. For your comfort and safety, remain seated with your seatbelt fastened until the aircraft has come to complete stop and the seat belt sign has been switched off. For those of you who would like to use your mobile phone, it is now safe to do so.

Before leaving the aircraft, make sure you take all personal belongings with you. Check your seat pocket and the overhead locker.

If you are transferring to another flight and need assistance, please contact the Airport Services staff meeting this flight.

I would like to thank you for choosing ____________ airlines. I hope that you have enjoyed your flight and look forward to seeing you again soon.

Good morning / afternoon / evening.

7. 동남아 항공사 A

1) Welcome announcement

Good morning / afternoon / evening, Ladies and Gentlemen.

My name is ____________, the Purser of this flight.

On behalf of __________ airlines, Capt __________ and the entire crew are very happy to welcome you on board this 비행기 기종 [B747, A330 etc]

This is non-smoking Flight 항공 편명.

The flight time to __________ will be _____hour(s) and _____minute(s)

In accordance with Civil Aviation Safety Regulation we will

① show you a video concerning the flight safety features of this aircraft.
② demonstrate the use of safety equipments and procedures of this aircraft.
Please fasten your seatbelt, adjust your seatback into upright position and lock your table securely.

2) After take off

Ladies and Gentlemen,
The FASTEN SEAT BELT sign if off now, but we recommend that you keep your seat belt comfortably fastened while seated.
In accordance with international Civil Aviation Organization Regulation, all lavatories no longer equipped with oxygen system. Should there be a sudden drop in cabin pressure, for passenger who use lavatory, please return to your seat and fasten your seatbelt.
Thank you.

3) Before Landing

Ladies and Gentlemen.
Shorty, we will be landing at _______ airport in _______.
The local time now is ____am/pm.
The time in _______ is ____hour(s) ahead of/behind 출발지.
There is no time difference between _________ and _________.
The ground temperature is _________ degrees Celsius.
Please fasten your seat belt, adjust your seatback into the upright position, and lock your table securely, stow your footrest and video monitor in place.
Also, keep your window shades open during this time.
Passengers using laptops and other entertainment devices, please switch them off now.
Thank you.

4) After landing

Ladies and Gentlemen,

We have just landed at ____________ (international) airport. Welcome to ____________.

Please remain seated until we have reached our final parking position and the FASTEN SEAT BELT sign is OFF.

Please do not switch on your cellular phone, until you are in the terminal building.

Before disembarking, please check your hand luggage.

We would like to remind you that you must be careful when you are opening the luggage bins.

Thank you.

8. 동남아 항공사 B

1) Welcome announcement

Good morning / afternoon / evening Ladies and Gentlemen.

Welcome aboard ____________ Airlines Flight _________ to _________.

The commander of this flight is Capt ________, I am (name) your (rank).

Our flight to ________ will take _____hours _____minutes.

For your safety, place your cabin luggage in the overhead compartment or under the seat in front of you. Do be careful whenever you open the overhead compartment.

For take off, put your seat upright, fasten your seatbelt and do not smoke.

The use of cellular telephones, CD players and pagers is prohibited.

Please refer to our crew for advice on the use of other electronic devices, as certain equipment may interfere with the aircraft systems.

We wish to remind you that smoking is not permitted on this flight.

Thank you.

2) After take-off

Ladies and Gentlemen,
The seat belt sigh is now off. For your safety, Please keep your seat belt fastened whenever you are seated.
Breakfast / lunch / dinner will be served shortly / in about _____minutes.
Please call us for any assistance.
Thank you.

3) Before landing

Ladies and Gentlemen.
We will be landing shortly.
Please put your seat upright, fasten your seatbelt and return your table to its original position.
Passengers disembarking at _____, please ensure that you have completed your disembarkation cards.
Thank you.

4) After landing

Ladies and Gentlemen.
We have landed at __________ (name of airport) __________ (city).
Please remain seated until the seatbelt sign is switched off.
The local time is ____am/pm, _____ (day), _____ (date), _______ (month), and the temperature is _____ degrees Celsius or _____ degrees Fahrenheit.
If you need any assistance on arrival, please contact our ground staff.
It has been a pleasure having you on board and we look forward to serving you again soon.
Thank you for flying with us and have a pleasant day / Goon night.

Reference

김시현, 이석만, 조영신(2009), Airline Service English, 한올출판사
김장춘, 임현빈(2001), Airline English(항공영어), 대광서림
박혜정(2010), 항공객실업무, 백산출판사
이동희, 권도희(2010), 항공실무영어, 새로미
이지민(2011), 항공객실 서비스론, 연경문화사
조선이(2010) 항공객실서비스 실무, 백산출판사
차석빈(2007), 펼치면 항공영어가 보인다(Airline Service English), 백산출판사
한정혜, 민정원, 서리(2011), 항공객실업무론, 집중과 선택
Sue ellis, Lewis Landsford(2010), English for Cabin Crew, OXFORD

Practice 정답

Practice 1.

1. May
2. check in
3. window
4. boarding
5. aisle
6. passport

Practice 2.

1. boarding
2. bags
3. back
4. as soon as possible
5. mind
6. anything
7. fragile
8. cabin
9. lavatory

Practice 3.

1. together
2. May
3. let / me
4. arranged
5. occupied
6. mistake
7. inconvenience
8. immediately

Practice 4.

1. aisle
2. hang
3. keep
4. under
5. pleasant
6. like
7. taking off

Practice 5.

1. help
2. change
3. informed
4. help
5. refer

Practice 6.

1. fastening
2. returning / upright position
3. closing
4. must ask

5. open
6. under
7. regulation

Practice 7

1. finished / with
2. may
3. rest
4. would / care
5. use
6. charge
7. free / charge

Practice 8

1. like
2. kind
3. would
4. care for
5. cup of
6. how
7. all
8. weak
9. inconvenience
10. afraid

Practice 9

1. take
2. another
3. yet
4. enjoy
5. preparation

Practice 10

1. return, upright, position
2. prefer
3. tray, table
4. mind
5. serving
6. run, out
7. moment, what, can
8. instead
9. else

Practice 11

1. serve
2. during
3. offer
4. heat
5. immediately
6. preparing
7. reservation, requested
8. accept
9. check
10. enjoy

Practice 12

1. have
2. need

3. enough
4. would
5. serve
6. meal, tray
7. hear
8. take

Practice 13

1. kind
2. right, after
3. order
4. hear
5. bother
6. willing
7. occupied

Practice 14

1. closing
2. hesitate
3. turn, on
4. press
5. come

Practice 15

1. purchase
2. allowed
3. signature
4. bring
5. change
6. sold, out
7. preparing

Practice 16

1. fill, out
2. like
3. need
4. leaving
5. version
6. staying

Practice 17

1. May
2. Is
3. about
4. difference, between
5. ahead

Practice 18

1. transportation, available
2. takes, about
3. how, long
4. recommend
5. exchange, rate

Practice 19

1. fastening
2. flight
3. shortly

4. fall off
5. flying
6. on board
7. keeping
8. safer

Practice 20

1. passport
2. purpose
3. got
4. trip
5. long
6. may
7. enjoy

Practice 21

1. claim
2. conveyor
3. help
4. tag
5. check / left
6. repaired
7. sorry

Practice 22

1. declare
2. customs declaration form
3. have
4. open

Practice 23

1. get
2. vomit
3. feeling
4. tried
5. blocked

Practice 24

1. few / more
2. take
3. loaded
4. as soon as

Practice 25

1. put out / step out
2. against
3. strictly
4. turn / off
5. cooperation
6. effects

Practice 26

1. like
2. lie down
3. pass / through
4. deck
5. knob
6. press
7. recline, lean back

저자소개

Siun Jung

세종대학교 대학원 관광경영 석사과정
전) 말레이시아 항공승무원
대한항공 국내선 사무장
KLM 네덜란드 항공사 객실승무원
산업인력공단 외국항공사 면접관
현) 장안대학교 항공운항과 교수
서울여자대학교 인재개발 아카데미 항공사 승무원 양성과정 교수
Able &Company 원장

Jeanhyo Ko

중국 상해 동화대학교 경영학 석사
전) 말레이시아 항공 객실승무원
국제매너센타 전임강사
현) Able &Company 대표
강남대학교 항공서비스경영학부 교수
서울여자대학교 인재개발 아카데미 항공사 승무원 양성과정 교수

Practical Airline Service English

2013년 2월 25일 초판 1쇄 인쇄
2013년 2월 28일 초판 1쇄 발행

저 자 정시은·고진효
발행인 寅製 진 욱 상
발행처 백산출판사

저자와의 합의하에 인지첩부 생략

서울시 성북구 정릉3동 653-40
등록 : 1974. 1. 9. 제 1-72호
전화 : 914-1621, 917-6240
FAX : 912-4438
http://www.ibaeksan.kr
editbsp@naver.com

값 14,000원
ISBN 978-89-6183-708-8